Session 1
90 Questions

1. According to the CFA Institute Code of Ethics and Standards of Professional Conduct, which of the following is not a duty to clients?

A. Loyalty
B. Fair dealing
C. Confidentiality
D. Honesty

2. Which of the following is not a component of Standard I: Professionalism?

A. Misrepresentation
B. Confidentiality
C. Professionalism
D. Independence and Objectivity

3. According to the guidance for Standard I(B): Independence and Objectivity, which of the following is a violation of the standard?

A. Accepting gifts from a client.
B. Providing objective and unbiased advice.
C. Disclosing all conflicts of interest.
D. Allowing personal biases to influence investment recommendations.

4. According to the guidance for Standard II(A): Material Nonpublic Information, which of the following actions is prohibited?

A. Trading on material nonpublic information obtained through legitimate channels.
B. Trading on material nonpublic information obtained through illegal channels.
C. Sharing material nonpublic information with other investment professionals.
D. All of the above.

5. Which of the following is not a requirement of Standard III(A): Loyalty, Prudence, and Care?

A. Acting in the best interests of clients.
B. Using reasonable judgment.
C. Conducting thorough research and analysis.
D. Providing guarantees of investment performance.

6. According to the guidance for Standard III(B): Fair Dealing, which of the following actions is prohibited?

A. Treating all clients equally.
B. Providing preferential treatment to high net worth clients.
C. Treating clients in a manner that is consistent with their objectives.
D. All of the above.

7. Which of the following is a requirement of Standard IV(A): Duties to Employers?

A. Maintaining confidentiality of employer information.
B. Disclosing all potential conflicts of interest.
C. Refraining from competing with the employer.
D. Adhering to the employer's code of ethics.

8. According to the guidance for Standard IV(B): Responsibilities of Supervisors, which of the following actions is required of supervisors?

A. Ensuring all employees comply with local laws and regulations.
B. Reviewing investment recommendations made by employees.

C. Providing investment advice to clients.
D. Allowing employees to act independently.

9. Which of the following is a requirement of Standard V(A): Diligence and Reasonable Basis?

A. Conducting thorough research and analysis.
B. Providing guarantees of investment performance.
C. Maintaining confidentiality of client information.
D. Providing investment recommendations based on personal opinions.

10. According to the guidance for Standard I(A): Knowledge of the Law, which of the following actions is required of investment professionals?

A. Adhering to all local laws and regulations.
B. Disclosing all potential conflicts of interest.
C. Maintaining confidentiality of client information.
D. Providing guarantees of investment performance.

11. According to the guidance for Standard I(B): Independence and Objectivity, which of the following actions is required of investment professionals?

A. Avoiding all conflicts of interest.
B. Providing investment recommendations based on personal opinions.
C. Disclosing all potential conflicts of interest.
D. Providing preferential treatment to high net worth clients.

12. According to the guidance for Standard II(A): Material Nonpublic Information, which of the following actions is prohibited?

A. Sharing material nonpublic information with other investment professionals.
B. Trading on material nonpublic information obtained through legitimate channels.

C. Providing investment recommendations based on material nonpublic information.
D. All of the above.

13. According to the guidance for Standard II(B): Market Manipulation, which of the following actions is prohibited?

A. Engaging in activities that may artificially inflate market prices.
B. Disclosing material nonpublic information to the public.
C. Providing false or misleading information to the public.
D. Allowing personal biases to influence investment recommendations.

14. According to the guidance for Standard III(A): Loyalty, Prudence, and Care, which of the following actions is required of investment professionals?

A. Providing guarantees of investment performance.
B. Disclosing all potential conflicts of interest.
C. Acting in the best interests of clients.
D. Providing preferential treatment to high net worth clients.

15. According to the guidance for Standard III(B): Fair Dealing, which of the following actions is prohibited?

A. Treating all clients equally.
B. Providing preferential treatment to high net worth clients.
C. Disclosing all potential conflicts of interest.
D. Providing investment recommendations based on personal opinions.

16. According to the guidance for Standard III(C): Suitability, which of the following actions is required of investment professionals?

A. Providing investment recommendations that are consistent with a client's objectives.
B. Providing investment recommendations based on personal opinions.

C. Providing investment recommendations that are consistent with the investment professional's interests.
D. Allowing personal biases to influence investment recommendations.

17. According to the guidance for Standard IV(B): Additional Compensation Arrangements, which of the following actions is prohibited?

A. Disclosing all potential conflicts of interest.
B. Entering into compensation arrangements that may create conflicts of interest.
C. Reporting compensation arrangements to the employer.
D. Providing investment recommendations based on personal opinions.

18. According to the guidance for Standard V(A): Diligence and Reasonable Basis, which of the following actions is required of investment professionals?

A. Conducting appropriate due diligence on all investments.
B. Providing investment recommendations based on personal opinions.
C. Focusing solely on quantitative analysis when evaluating investments.
D. Providing guarantees of investment performance.

19. According to the guidance for Standard V(B): Communication with Clients and Prospective Clients, which of the following actions is required of investment professionals?

A. Disclosing all potential conflicts of interest.
B. Providing investment recommendations that are consistent with the investment professional's interests.
C. Making investment recommendations without considering a client's objectives.
D. Guaranteeing a specific investment outcome.

20. According to the guidance for Standard VI(A): Disclosure of Conflicts, which of the following actions is required of investment professionals?

A. Disclosing all potential conflicts of interest.
B. Providing preferential treatment to high net worth clients.
C. Disclosing only material conflicts of interest.
D. Providing investment recommendations based on personal opinions.

21. According to the guidance for Standard VI(B): Priority of Transactions, which of the following actions is prohibited?

A. Prioritizing client transactions over the investment professional's own transactions.
B. Failing to disclose potential conflicts of interest related to transaction priority.
C. Focusing solely on short-term investment performance when prioritizing transactions.
D. Providing investment recommendations based on personal opinions.

22. According to the guidance for Standard VII(A): Conduct as Members and Candidates in the CFA Program, which of the following actions is prohibited?

A. Cheating on the CFA exam.
B. Providing investment recommendations based on personal opinions.
C. Failing to disclose potential conflicts of interest.
D. Disclosing confidential information about the CFA exam.

23. According to the guidance for Standard III(B): Fair Dealing, which of the following actions is prohibited?

A. Disclosing all potential conflicts of interest.
B. Engaging in insider trading.

C. Providing preferential treatment to high net worth clients.
D. Making investment recommendations without considering a client's objectives.

24. What is the purpose of the Global Investment Performance Standards (GIPS)?

A. To establish ethical standards for investment professionals.
B. To provide a framework for calculating and presenting investment performance.
C. To regulate the global investment industry.
D. To provide guidelines for risk management.

25. Which of the following firms is required to comply with the GIPS standards?

A. A private equity firm.
B. A hedge fund.
C. A mutual fund.
D. A real estate investment trust (REIT).

26. Which of the following is an important benefit of GIPS compliance for investment firms?

A. Improved risk management.
B. Higher returns for investors.
C. Reduced legal liability.
D. Increased transparency and credibility.

27. Which of the following is a requirement for a firm to claim compliance with the GIPS standards?

A. The firm must disclose all conflicts of interest.
B. The firm must have a code of ethics in place.
C. The firm must have at least 10 years of investment performance data.
D. The firm must have a third-party verification of its compliance.

28. What is the future value of an investment of $10,000 if it earns an annual interest rate of 8%, compounded quarterly, for 5 years?

A. $14,693
B. $15,466
C. $14,859
D. $17,052

29. What is the present value of a $5,000 payment to be received in 8 years if the discount rate is 6%?

A. $2,946
B. $3137
C. $3,364
D. $3,573

30. Which of the following measures of central tendency is most affected by extreme values?

A. Mean
B. Median
C. Mode

31. Which of the following measures of dispersion is most affected by extreme values?

A. Range
B. Interquartile range
C. Standard deviation

32. Which of the following graphs is best used for comparing the frequency distribution of two datasets?

A. Histogram
B. Line chart
C. Scatter plot

33. A stock has a 70% chance of returning 10% and a 30% chance of returning -5%. What is the expected return of the stock?

A. 7%
B. 6.5%
C. 5.5%

34. A company has two factories that produce a certain product. Factory A produces 60% of the product and factory B produces 40% of the product. Of the product produced by factory A, 5% is defective, while of the product produced by factory B, 8% is defective. What is the probability that a randomly chosen product is defective?

A. 0.02
B. 0.05
C. 0.056
D. 0.068

35. An analyst estimates that there is a 20% chance that a company will report higher than expected earnings, a 30% chance that it will report earnings in line with expectations, and a 50% chance that it will report lower than expected earnings. If the stock is expected to increase by 10% if earnings are higher than expected, decrease by 5% if earnings are in line with expectations, and decrease by 15% if earnings are lower than expected, what is the expected return on the stock?

A. -2.5%
B. 5.5%
C. -4%
D. -7%

36. An investor has a portfolio of two stocks, Stock A and Stock B. The probability of Stock A increasing in value on any given day is 0.6, and the probability of Stock B increasing in

value on any given day is 0.4. What is the probability that at least one of the stocks will increase in value on a given day?

A. 0.24
B. 0.76
C. 0.82

37. A company produces widgets with a mean weight of 10 grams and a standard deviation of 2 grams. What is the probability that a randomly selected widget will weigh between 8 and 12 grams?

A. 0.3413
B. 0.4772
C. 0.6827

38. A distribution has a kurtosis of 3. This indicates that the distribution is:

A. platykurtic
B. leptokurtic
C. mesokurtic

39. Which of the following statements is true about the normal distribution?

A. It is symmetric and unimodal.
B. It is always positively skewed.
C. It has a kurtosis of zero.
D. It is a discrete distribution.

40. A sample of 50 households in a certain area shows an average annual income of $75,000 with a standard deviation of $10,000. What is the 95% confidence interval for the population mean income?

A. $71,352 to $78,648
B. $72,540 to $77,460
C. $73,228 to $76,772

41. A manager wants to estimate the mean time spent by employees on a certain task. A random sample of 25 employees is selected, and the mean time spent is 50 minutes with a standard deviation of 8 minutes. What is the standard error of the mean?

A. 1.6 minutes
B. 1.8 minutes
C. 2.0 minutes

42. A company is interested in estimating the proportion of its customers who are satisfied with its product. The company plans to conduct a survey and use the results to estimate the population proportion. Which of the following factors would increase the margin of error in the estimate?

A. Increasing the sample size
B. Increasing the confidence level
C. Decreasing the variability in the population
D. Using a stratified sampling technique

43. A mutual fund claims that its investment strategy generates higher returns than the market average. A hypothesis test is conducted to determine whether this claim is true. The null hypothesis is that the fund's returns are not higher than the market average. The alternative hypothesis is that the fund's returns are higher than the market average. The test produces a p-value of 0.025. What can be concluded from this result at a 95% confidence level?

A. The null hypothesis cannot be rejected at a 95% confidence level.
B. The alternative hypothesis cannot be rejected at a 95% confidence level.
C. There is insufficient evidence to support either the null hypothesis or the alternative hypothesis at a 95% confidence level.
D. The alternative hypothesis can be rejected at a 95% confidence level.

44. A company is investigating the effectiveness of a new training program designed to improve the sales performance of its employees. The null hypothesis is that the training program has no effect on sales performance. The alternative hypothesis is that the training program has a positive effect on sales performance. The test produces a p-value of 0.02. What can be concluded from this result at a 95% confidence level?

A. There is insufficient evidence to support either the null hypothesis or the alternative hypothesis at a 95% confidence level.
B. The alternative hypothesis can be rejected at a 95% confidence level.
C. The null hypothesis can be rejected at a 95% confidence level.
D. The p-value is not significant enough to make any conclusion at a 95% confidence level.

45. A portfolio manager wants to estimate the relationship between a stock's returns and the returns of the market as a whole. She collects monthly return data for the stock and the market over the past two years and runs a simple linear regression model using the least squares method. The resulting regression equation is Y = 0.8X + 0.02, where Y is the stock's returns and X is the market returns. What is the predicted stock return if the market return for the current month is 2.5%?

A. 0.58%
B. 1.10%
C. 2.22%
D. 2.02%

46. If the demand for a product is perfectly inelastic, what is the value of the price elasticity of demand?

A. 0
B. 0.5
C. 1.0
D. Infinity

47. If the demand for a product is perfectly elastic, which of the following is true?

A. A small increase in price will cause a large decrease in quantity demanded.
B. A small decrease in price will cause a large increase in quantity demanded.
C. A large increase in price will cause a small decrease in quantity demanded.
D. A large decrease in price will cause a small increase in quantity demanded.

48. Which of the following is NOT a characteristic of perfect competition?

A. A large number of buyers and sellers
B. Homogeneous products
C. Free entry and exit of firms in the industry
D. Individual firms have some control over the price of their product

49. Which of the following is a characteristic of a monopolistically competitive market structure?

A. A large number of buyers and sellers
B. Homogeneous products
C. Free entry and exit of firms in the industry
D. Product differentiation

50. Which of the following is an example of an expansionary fiscal policy?

A. Increasing taxes
B. Reducing government spending
C. Decreasing interest rates
D. Increasing government spending

51. If the economy is experiencing high inflation and the central bank wants to reduce it, which of the following monetary policy actions is most likely to be implemented?

A. Decreasing interest rates
B. Increasing government spending
C. Increasing taxes
D. Increasing the reserve requirement

52. If an economy is experiencing a recessionary gap, which of the following fiscal policy actions is most appropriate to close the gap and stimulate economic growth?

A. Decreasing taxes
B. Increasing government spending
C. Increasing interest rates
D. Reducing the money supply

53. During which phase of the business cycle is the economy characterized by high levels of economic activity, high employment rates, and increasing inflation?

A. Expansion
B. Peak
C. Contraction
D. Trough

54. During the expansion phase of a credit cycle, which of the following is most likely to occur?

A. Lenders tighten credit standards and reduce lending.
B. Borrowers experience difficulty in repaying their loans.
C. Interest rates decrease, making borrowing more affordable.
D. Credit spreads widen, reflecting increased risk in lending.

55. Which of the following is a limitation of monetary policy compared to fiscal policy?

A. Monetary policy can be implemented quickly.
B. Monetary policy has a more direct impact on aggregate demand.
C. Monetary policy can address supply-side issues effectively.
D. Monetary policy is subject to time lags and uncertainty.

56. Which of the following is a primary objective of monetary policy?

A. Maintaining price stability
B. Managing government spending
C. Controlling fiscal deficits
D. Determining tax rates

57. Which of the following best describes the concept of fiscal policy?

A. Government actions that influence the money supply and interest rates in the economy.
B. Government actions that aim to stabilize the economy through changes in taxation and government spending.
C. Central bank actions that control inflation and stabilize the financial system.
D. Market-driven mechanisms that determine the allocation of resources in the economy.

58. Which of the following monetary policy regimes *most likely* imports the inflation of a foreign economy?

A. Inflation targeting
B. Interest rate targeting
C. Exchange rate targeting

59. Which of the following is an example of a tariff barrier to international trade?

A. Subsidies provided by a government to domestic industries.
B. An import quota imposed on a specific product.
C. Intellectual property rights protection for foreign investors.
D. The establishment of regional trade agreements.

60. Which of the following factors promotes international trade?

A. High trade barriers and protectionist policies.
B. Currency devaluation and exchange rate controls.

C. Political instability and conflicts.
D. Comparative advantage and specialization.

61. Which of the following is an example of a capital flow in the international financial system?

A. A country importing goods and services from abroad.
B. An individual purchasing foreign stocks and bonds.
C. A government imposing tariffs on imported goods.
D. A company exporting products to foreign markets.

62. The spot exchange rate between the U.S. dollar (USD) and the Canadian dollar (CAD) is 1 USD = 1.25 CAD. If the Canadian dollar appreciates by 10% against the U.S. dollar, what is the new exchange rate?

A. 1 USD = 1.35 CAD
B. 1 USD = 1.15 CAD
C. 1 USD = 1.375 CAD
D. 1 USD = 1.125 CAD

63. Which of the following exchange rate systems involves a fixed exchange rate with periodic adjustments?

A. Floating exchange rate system.
B. Managed float exchange rate system.
C. Crawling peg exchange rate system.
D. Free float exchange rate system.

64. A company has current assets of $500,000, current liabilities of $300,000, long-term assets of $700,000, and long-term liabilities of $400,000. What is the company's net working capital?

A. $100,000
B. $200,000
C. $300,000
D. $500,000

65. Under International Financial Reporting Standards (IFRS), which of the following is a characteristic of a finance lease?

A. The leased asset is not recorded on the lessee's balance sheet.
B. The lease payments are recognized as operating expenses.
C. The lease term is less than one year.
D. The lessee assumes substantially all the risks and rewards of ownership.

66. A company reported revenue of $1,000,000, cost of goods sold of $600,000, and operating expenses of $200,000. What is the company's gross profit?

A. $400,000
B. $200,000
C. $800,000
D. $300,000

67. Which of the following statements is true regarding the income statement?

A. It provides information about a company's financial position at a specific point in time.
B. It presents a summary of cash inflows and outflows during a given period.
C. It reports a company's revenues, expenses, and net income over a specific period.
D. It discloses changes in a company's equity during a reporting period.

68. A company reported the following information for the year:

- Revenue: $1,500,000
- Cost of Goods Sold: $600,000
- Selling and Administrative Expenses: $300,000
- Interest Income: $50,000
- Interest Expense: $20,000
- Income Tax Expense: $100,000

Calculate the company's operating profit margin.
A. 33.33%
B. 40.00%
C. 46.67%
D. 50.00%

69. A company's balance sheet shows the following information:

- Cash: $100,000
- Accounts Receivable: $200,000
- Inventory: $150,000
- Property, Plant, and Equipment: $600,000
- Total Assets: $1,200,000
- Accounts Payable: $100,000
- Notes Payable: $200,000
- Long-Term Debt: $400,000
- Total Liabilities: $700,000
- Shareholders' Equity: $500,000

Calculate the company's current ratio.
A. 1.5
B. 2.0
C. 1.0
D. 0.67

70. A company has total assets of $2,500,000, total liabilities of $1,200,000, and shareholders' equity of $1,300,000. What is the company's debt-to-equity ratio?

A. 0.92
B. 1.46
C. 0.92%
D. 1.46%

71. Which of the following is considered a cash inflow from operating activities in the cash flow statement?

A. Payment of dividends to shareholders
B. Purchase of property, plant, and equipment

C. Receipt of interest income
D. Issuance of long-term debt

72. Which section of the cash flow statement includes cash flows related to the purchase and sale of long-term assets?

A. Operating activities
B. Investing activities
C. Financing activities
D. Non-cash activities

73. Which of the following cash flow ratios measures a company's ability to generate sufficient cash flow to cover its debt obligations?

A. Operating cash flow margin
B. Cash flow return on investment
C. Cash flow yield
D. Cash flow coverage ratio

74. A company reported the following information for the year:

- Net income: $500,000
- Depreciation expense: $100,000
- Increase in accounts receivable: $50,000
- Increase in accounts payable: $20,000
- Purchase of property, plant, and equipment: $150,000

Calculate the company's cash flow from operating activities using the indirect method.
A. $680,000
B. $570,000
C. $450,000
D. $520,000

75. A company has an earnings per share (EPS) of $2.50, a price/earnings (P/E) ratio of 15, and a dividend payout ratio of 40%. What is the company's dividend per share?

A. $0.50
B. $1.00
C. $1.25
D. $2.00

76. A company has a total debt of $1,000,000 and total equity of $2,500,000. Its debt-to-equity ratio is 0.8. What is the company's total assets?

A. $1,500,000
B. $2,000,000
C. $3,000,000
D. $3,750,000

77. ABC Company has a net profit of $500,000 and total assets of $5,000,000. The average total assets for the industry are $10,000,000. Compared to the industry average, the company's ROA:

A. Lower than the industry average
B. The same as industry average
C. Higher than industry average

78. Which of the following inventory valuation methods is not permitted under International Financial Reporting Standards (IFRS)?

A. LIFO (Last In, First Out)
B. FIFO (First In, First Out)
C. Weighted Average Cost
D. Specific Identification

79. The inventory turnover ratio is calculated by dividing:

A. Cost of Goods Sold by Ending Inventory
B. Sales Revenue by Average Inventory
C. Ending Inventory by Cost of Goods Sold
D. Average Inventory by Sales Revenue

80. ABC Company uses the FIFO (First In, First Out) method for inventory valuation. In a period of rising prices, which of the following statements is true?

A. Cost of Goods Sold will be higher compared to LIFO.
B. Ending inventory will be lower compared to LIFO.
C. Gross profit will be lower compared to LIFO.
D. Net income will be higher compared to LIFO.

81. A company has a beginning inventory of $100,000, purchases of $300,000, sales of $400,000, and an ending inventory of $150,000. What is the inventory turnover ratio?

A. 0.75
B. 1.33
C. 2.67
D. 3.2

82. Which of the following is NOT a tangible long-lived asset?

A. Buildings
B. Machinery and equipment
C. Patents
D. Land

83. XYZ Company purchased a patent for $500,000. The patent has a remaining legal life of 10 years and an estimated economic life of 15 years. If the company follows the straight-line amortization method for intangible assets, what is the annual amortization expense for the patent?

A. $33,333
B. $35,000
C. $45,000
D. $50,000

84. ABC Company acquired a piece of machinery for $200,000. The machinery has a useful life of 8 years and an estimated residual value of $20,000. If the company uses the double-

declining balance method of depreciation, what is the depreciation expense for Year 2?

A. $31,250
B. $37,500
C. $40,000
D. $50,000

85. Which of the following methods of calculating depreciation results in a higher depreciation expense in the earlier years of an asset's life?

A. Straight-line method
B. Double-declining balance method
C. Units-of-production method

86. Which of the following statements regarding deferred tax liabilities is correct?

A. Deferred tax liabilities result in an increase in future tax payments.
B. Deferred tax liabilities arise when tax expenses exceed tax payments.
C. Deferred tax liabilities are recognized when tax assets are greater than tax liabilities.
D. Deferred tax liabilities decrease future taxable income.

87. ABC Company has a deferred tax asset of $50,000 and a deferred tax liability of $30,000 on its balance sheet. Which of the following statements is true regarding the net presentation of these deferred tax items?

A. The deferred tax asset and deferred tax liability should be offset against each other, resulting in a net deferred tax liability of $20,000.
B. The deferred tax asset and deferred tax liability should be reported separately on the balance sheet.
C. The deferred tax asset should be reported as an offset against income taxes payable, and the deferred tax liability should be reported as a separate liability.

D. The deferred tax asset and deferred tax liability should be offset against each other, resulting in a net deferred tax asset of $20,000.

88. XYZ Company issued a $1,000,000 bond with a coupon rate of 6% and a maturity period of 5 years. The bond pays interest semi-annually. What is the semi-annual interest payment associated with this bond?

A. $30,000
B. $15,000
C. $60,000
D. $10,000

89. Which of the following indicators is typically associated with higher financial reporting quality?

A. Higher earnings management
B. Lower transparency in financial disclosures
C. Higher accruals quality
D. Lower auditor independence

90. Company ABC and Company XYZ operate in the same industry. ABC Company has a higher current ratio compared to XYZ Company. Which of the following statements is most likely true?

A. ABC Company has a more favorable liquidity position than XYZ Company.
B. XYZ Company has a more favorable liquidity position than ABC Company.
C. ABC Company has a higher debt-to-equity ratio than XYZ Company.
D. XYZ Company has a higher debt-to-equity ratio than ABC Company.

Session 1
Answers

Answers:

1. Answer: D. Honesty is not a duty to clients under the CFA Institute Code of Ethics and Standards of Professional Conduct, but rather a basic ethical principle.

2. Answer: A. Misrepresentation is not a component of Standard I: Professionalism.
3. Answer: D. Allowing personal biases to influence investment recommendations is a violation of Standard I(B): Independence and Objectivity.
4. Answer: B. Trading on material nonpublic information obtained through illegal channels is prohibited under Standard II(A): Material Nonpublic Information.
5. Answer: D. Providing guarantees of investment performance is not a requirement of Standard III(A): Loyalty, Prudence, and Care.
6. Answer: B. Providing preferential treatment to high net worth clients is prohibited under Standard III(B): Fair Dealing.
7. Answer: A. Maintaining confidentiality of employer information is a requirement of Standard IV(A): Duties to Employers.
8. Answer: B. Reviewing investment recommendations made by employees is required of supervisors under Standard IV(B): Responsibilities of Supervisors.
9. Answer: A. Conducting thorough research and analysis is a requirement of Standard V(A): Diligence and Reasonable Basis.
10. Answer: A. Adhering to all local laws and regulations is required of investment professionals under Standard I(A): Knowledge of the Law.
11. Answer: C. Disclosing all potential conflicts of interest is required of investment professionals under Standard I(B): Independence and Objectivity.
12. Answer: C. Providing investment recommendations based on material nonpublic information is prohibited under Standard II(A): Material Nonpublic Information.
13. Answer: A. Engaging in activities that may artificially inflate market prices is prohibited under Standard II(B): Market Manipulation.
14. Answer: C. Acting in the best interests of clients is required of investment professionals under Standard III(A): Loyalty, Prudence, and Care.

15. Answer: B. Providing preferential treatment to high net worth clients is prohibited under Standard III(B): Fair Dealing.
16. Answer: A. Providing investment recommendations that are consistent with a client's objectives is required of investment professionals under Standard III(C): Suitability.
17. Answer: B. Entering into compensation arrangements that may create conflicts of interest is prohibited under Standard IV(B): Additional Compensation Arrangements.
18. Answer: A. Conducting appropriate due diligence on all investments is required of investment professionals under Standard V(A): Diligence and Reasonable Basis.
19. Answer: A. Disclosing all potential conflicts of interest is required of investment professionals under Standard V(B): Communication with Clients and Prospective Clients.
20. Answer: A. Disclosing all potential conflicts of interest is required of investment professionals under Standard VI(A): Disclosure of Conflicts.
21. Answer: B. Failing to disclose potential conflicts of interest related to transaction priority is prohibited under Standard VI(B): Priority of Transactions.
22. Answer: A. Cheating on the CFA exam is prohibited under Standard VII(A): Conduct as Members and Candidates in the CFA Program.
23. Answer: B. Engaging in insider trading is prohibited under Standard III(B): Fair Dealing.
24. Answer: B. The purpose of the Global Investment Performance Standards (GIPS) is to provide a framework for calculating and presenting investment performance.
25. Answer: C. A mutual fund is required to comply with the GIPS standards, while compliance is voluntary for other types of investment firms.
26. Answer: D. An important benefit of GIPS compliance for investment firms is increased transparency and credibility, which can help attract new clients and retain existing ones.
27. Answer: D. A requirement for a firm to claim compliance with the GIPS standards is that it must have a third-party verification of its compliance.

28. Answer: C. The future value of an investment that earns an annual interest rate of 8%, compounded quarterly, for 5 years is calculated as $FV = PV \times (1 + r/n)^{(n \times t)}$, where PV is the present value, r is the interest rate, n is the number of compounding periods per year, and t is the number of years. Plugging in the numbers, we get $FV = \$10,000 \times (1 + 0.08/4)^{(4 \times 5)} = \$14,859.47$.
29. Answer: B. The present value of a future cash flow is calculated as $PV = FV / (1 + r)^n$, where FV is the future value, r is the discount rate, and n is the number of years. Plugging in the numbers, we get $PV = \$5,000 / (1 + 0.06)^8 = \$3137.06$.
30. Answer: A. The mean is the arithmetic average of a set of values, and is calculated by adding up all the values and dividing by the total number of values. It is highly sensitive to extreme values because it takes into account all the values in the dataset, including outliers. Therefore, the mean can be significantly affected by extreme values, which can distort its value.
31. Answer: C. The standard deviation measures the dispersion of a set of values around the mean. It takes into account all the values in the dataset, including outliers. As such, extreme values can have a significant impact on the standard deviation, causing it to increase or decrease depending on the direction of the outlier. In contrast, the range and interquartile range are less sensitive to extreme values.
32. Answer: A. A histogram is a graph that displays the frequency distribution of a set of data. It consists of a series of adjacent rectangles, where the width of each rectangle represents the interval of values and the height represents the frequency of observations within that interval. A histogram is particularly useful for comparing the frequency distributions of two or more datasets, as it allows for a visual comparison of the shape, central tendency, and dispersion of each distribution.
33. Answer: C. The expected return of the stock is calculated by multiplying each possible return by its probability and summing the results. In this case, the expected return is:

Expected return = (0.7 x 0.10) + (0.3 x -0.05) = 0.07 - 0.015 = 0.055 = 5.5%

34. Answer: C. Explanation: Probability of choosing a defective product from Factory A = 0.60 x 0.05 = 0.03 Probability of choosing a defective product from Factory B = 0.40 x 0.08 = 0.032 Probability of choosing a defective product = 0.03 + 0.032 = 0.056

35. Answer: D. Explanation: Expected return = (0.20 x 0.10) + (0.30 x (-0.05)) + (0.50 x (-0.15)) = 0.02 - 0.015 - 0.075 = -0.07. Therefore, the expected return on the stock is -7%.

36. Answer: B. To calculate the probability that at least one of the stocks will increase in value on a given day, we can use the complement rule. The probability that neither stock will increase in value is: P(neither) = P(A does not increase) * P(B does not increase) = (1 - 0.6) * (1 - 0.4) = 0.4 * 0.6 = 0.24 Therefore, the probability that at least one of the stocks will increase in value is: P(at least one) = 1 - P(neither) = 1 - 0.24 = 0.76

37. Answer: C. Since the weight of widgets is normally distributed with a mean of 10 grams and a standard deviation of 2 grams, we can use the standard normal distribution to find the probability that a randomly selected widget will weigh between 8 and 12 grams. First, we need to standardize the values of 8 and 12 grams using the formula:
$z = (x - mean) / standard\ deviation$
So, z for 8 grams is:
$z = (8 - 10) / 2 = -1$
And z for 12 grams is:
$z = (12 - 10) / 2 = 1$
Next, we use a standard normal distribution table to find the area between z = -1 and z = 1, which is 0.6827. Therefore, the probability that a randomly selected widget will weigh between 8 and 12 grams is 0.6827.

38. Answer: B. Kurtosis measures the peakedness or flatness of a distribution relative to the normal distribution. A kurtosis of 3 indicates that the distribution is more peaked than the normal distribution (which has a kurtosis of 0), and is therefore leptokurtic.

39. Answer: A. It is symmetric and unimodal. The normal distribution, also known as the Gaussian distribution or the bell curve, is a continuous probability distribution that is characterized by its symmetric and unimodal shape. The curve is symmetric around its mean and has a bell-shaped appearance. It is not positively skewed, which means that its tail is not longer on the right side. The normal distribution has a kurtosis of zero, which means that it has the same level of peakedness as the standard normal distribution. It is a continuous distribution, which means that it can take on any value within a range, and is not a discrete distribution.
40. Answer: A. $71,352 to $78,648
    The 95% confidence interval for the population mean income can be calculated using the formula:
    $CI = X \pm (Z * SE)$
    where X is the sample mean, Z is the z-score corresponding to the level of confidence (95% in this case), and SE is the standard error of the mean, which is equal to the standard deviation of the sample divided by the square root of the sample size.
    So, the lower bound of the confidence interval is:
    $75,000 - (1.96 * (10,000 / \sqrt{50})) = \$71,352$
    And the upper bound of the confidence interval is:
    $75,000 + (1.96 * (10,000 / \sqrt{50})) = \$78,648$
    Therefore, the 95% confidence interval for the population mean income is $71,352 to $78,648.
41. Answer: A. 1.6 minutes The standard error of the mean is a measure of the variability of sample means, and can be calculated using the formula:
    $SE = s / \sqrt{n}$
    where s is the standard deviation of the sample and n is the sample size.
    In this case, we have:
    $SE = 8 / \sqrt{25} = 1.6$
    Therefore, the standard error of the mean is 1.6 minutes.
42. Answer: B. Increasing the confidence level. The margin of error in an estimate is influenced by several factors, including the level of confidence, the sample size, and the variability in the population. Increasing the sample size would decrease the

margin of error, as it would increase the precision of the estimate. Decreasing the variability in the population would also decrease the margin of error, as it would reduce the amount of uncertainty in the estimate. Using a stratified sampling technique can also reduce the margin of error by ensuring that the sample is representative of the population.

43. Answer: D. The alternative hypothesis can be rejected at a 95% confidence level.
44. Answer: C. The null hypothesis can be rejected at a 95% confidence level. Since the p-value (0.02) is less than the significance level of 0.05 (or 5%), there is sufficient evidence to reject the null hypothesis. This means that the training program does have a statistically significant positive effect on sales performance at a 95% confidence level. Therefore, we can conclude that the training program is effective in improving sales performance.
45. Answer: D. 2.02%. To solve the problem, we substitute $X = 2.5$ into the regression equation and solve for Y:
$Y = 0.8X + 0.02$
$Y = 0.8(2.5) + 0.02$
$Y = 2.00 + 0.02$
$Y = 2.02\%$
Therefore, the predicted stock return for the current month is 2.02%.
46. Answer: A. 0. If the demand for a product is perfectly inelastic, it means that the quantity demanded does not change at all in response to changes in price. Mathematically, this means that the price elasticity of demand is zero, because any percentage change in price will result in zero percentage change in quantity demanded. Therefore, the correct answer is A. 0.
47. Answer: B. A small decrease in price will cause a large increase in quantity demanded. If the demand for a product is perfectly elastic, it means that any increase in price will cause quantity demanded to fall to zero, and any decrease in price will cause quantity demanded to rise to infinity. In other words, demand is infinitely responsive to changes in price.

48. Answer: D. Individual firms have some control over the price of their product. Perfect competition is a market structure in which there are a large number of buyers and sellers, homogeneous products, and free entry and exit of firms in the industry. In perfect competition, no individual firm has any control over the price of its product, as the market price is determined by the interaction of supply and demand.
49. Answer: D. Product differentiation. Monopolistic competition is a market structure in which there are many buyers and sellers, free entry and exit of firms in the industry, and product differentiation. Product differentiation means that firms produce products that are slightly different from each other, so they are not perfect substitutes.
50. Answer: D. Increasing government spending. Expansionary fiscal policy refers to government actions that aim to stimulate economic growth and increase aggregate demand. One of the ways to implement expansionary fiscal policy is by increasing government spending. By increasing spending on public projects, infrastructure, or social programs, the government injects money into the economy, creating a multiplier effect that boosts aggregate demand and economic activity.
51. Answer: D. Increasing the reserve requirement. To combat high inflation, the central bank typically implements contractionary monetary policy. One tool available to the central bank is adjusting the reserve requirement, which is the percentage of deposits that banks are required to hold as reserves. By increasing the reserve requirement, the central bank reduces the amount of money available for lending and spending, which helps to reduce inflationary pressures.
52. Answer: B. Increasing government spending. During a recessionary gap, the economy is operating below its potential output level, indicating a lack of aggregate demand. To stimulate economic growth and close the gap, expansionary fiscal policy measures are required. One such measure is increasing government spending. By increasing government spending, more money is injected into the economy, stimulating aggregate demand and promoting economic growth.

53. Answer: B. Peak. The peak phase of the business cycle is the highest point of economic activity before a contraction or downturn begins. During this phase, the economy experiences high levels of economic activity, with high employment rates and increasing inflation. It is a period of strong economic growth and optimism. However, after the peak phase, the economy starts to slow down, leading to a contraction phase.
54. Answer: C. Interest rates decrease, making borrowing more affordable. During the expansion phase of a credit cycle, economic activity is generally robust, and credit availability tends to increase. This expansionary phase is characterized by improved economic conditions, higher borrower confidence, and increased demand for credit.
55. Answer: D. Monetary policy is subject to time lags and uncertainty. While monetary policy has its advantages, it also has limitations when compared to fiscal policy. One of the key limitations is that monetary policy is subject to time lags and uncertainty. Changes in monetary policy, such as interest rate adjustments, take time to affect the economy. Additionally, the transmission mechanisms of monetary policy can be unpredictable, leading to uncertainty in the outcomes.
56. Answer: A. Maintaining price stability. A primary objective of monetary policy is to maintain price stability. Central banks aim to keep inflation at a moderate and stable level to support overall economic stability and confidence. By managing interest rates, money supply, and other monetary tools, central banks work towards controlling inflation and preventing excessive price volatility.
57. Answer: B. Government actions that aim to stabilize the economy through changes in taxation and government spending. Fiscal policy refers to the use of government actions to influence the overall state of the economy. It involves making changes in taxation and government spending with the objective of stabilizing the economy, managing aggregate demand, and promoting economic growth. Through fiscal policy, the government can stimulate

or contract the economy to address issues such as inflation, unemployment, and economic fluctuations.
58. Answer: C. Exchange rate targeting. The idea behind exchange rate targeting is that by tying a domestic economy's currency to that of an economy with a good track record on inflation, the domestic economy would effectively import the inflation experience of the low inflation economy and t is in this sense that a successful exchange rate policy imports the inflation of the foreign economy.
59. Answer: B. An import quota imposed on a specific product. A tariff is a tax imposed on imported goods, making them more expensive and less competitive in the domestic market. An import quota, on the other hand, limits the quantity of a specific product that can be imported into a country. By restricting the quantity, an import quota effectively raises prices and reduces competition. Hence, an import quota is an example of a tariff barrier to international trade.
60. Answer: D. Comparative advantage and specialization. Comparative advantage refers to the ability of a country to produce a specific good or service at a lower opportunity cost compared to other countries. Specialization occurs when countries focus on producing goods or services in which they have a comparative advantage. These concepts promote international trade by allowing countries to specialize in the production of goods they are most efficient at, and then trade with other nations for goods they cannot produce as efficiently.
61. Answer: B. An individual purchasing foreign stocks and bonds. Capital flows refer to the movement of money and financial assets between countries. When an individual purchases foreign stocks and bonds, they are engaging in a capital flow by investing in financial assets outside of their home country. Capital flows can also include foreign direct investment (FDI) by companies, loans provided by international banks, and portfolio investments made by institutional investors.
62. Answer: C. 1 USD = 1.375 CAD. To calculate the new exchange rate, we need to increase the original exchange rate

by the appreciation percentage: 1.25 CAD + (1.25 CAD * 10%) = 1.25 CAD + 0.125 CAD = 1.375 CAD.
63. Answer: C. Crawling peg exchange rate system. A crawling peg exchange rate system involves a fixed exchange rate where the currency value is periodically adjusted or "crawls" in response to certain predetermined factors. The adjustments are usually made to control inflation or maintain competitiveness in international trade. The rate at which the exchange rate adjusts can be predetermined or determined by a formula.
64. Answer: B. $200,000. Net working capital represents the difference between current assets and current liabilities. It can be calculated using the formula:
Net Working Capital = Current Assets - Current Liabilities
Plugging in the given values:
Net Working Capital = $500,000 - $300,000 = $200,000
65. Answer: D. The lessee assumes substantially all the risks and rewards of ownership. Under IFRS, a finance lease is a lease that transfers substantially all the risks and rewards of ownership to the lessee. The lessee is effectively treated as the owner of the leased asset and records it on their balance sheet. The lease payments are split into principal and interest components, with the interest portion recognized as an expense and the principal portion reducing the lease liability over time.
66. Answer: A. $400,000. Gross profit is calculated by subtracting the cost of goods sold from revenue:
Gross Profit = Revenue - Cost of Goods Sold
Plugging in the given values:
Gross Profit = $1,000,000 - $600,000 = $400,000
Therefore, the correct answer is A. $400,000.
67. Answer: C. It reports a company's revenues, expenses, and net income over a specific period. The income statement, also known as the statement of comprehensive income, reports a company's revenues, expenses, and net income over a specific period, such as a month, quarter, or year. It provides information about a company's financial performance, specifically the profitability of its operations, by presenting the revenues earned and the expenses incurred

during that period. The net income is calculated by subtracting total expenses from total revenues.

68. Answer: B. 40.00%. The operating profit margin is a profitability ratio that measures a company's operating income as a percentage of its revenue. It is calculated using the formula:
Operating Profit Margin = (Operating Income / Revenue) * 100
To find the operating income, we subtract the cost of goods sold and selling/administrative expenses from the revenue:
Operating Income = Revenue - Cost of Goods Sold - Selling/Administrative Expenses
Operating Income = $1,500,000 - $600,000 - $300,000
Operating Income = $600,000
Now we can calculate the operating profit margin:
Operating Profit Margin = ($600,000 / $1,500,000) * 100
Operating Profit Margin = 0.40 * 100
Operating Profit Margin = 40.00%

69. Answer: A. 1.5. The current ratio is calculated by dividing total current assets by total current liabilities:
Current Ratio = Total Current Assets / Total Current Liabilities
Plugging in the given values:
Current Ratio = $450,000 / $300,000
Current Ratio = 1.5

70. Answer: A. 0.92. The debt-to-equity ratio is calculated by dividing total liabilities by shareholders' equity:
Debt-to-Equity Ratio = Total Liabilities / Shareholders' Equity
Plugging in the given values:
Debt-to-Equity Ratio = $1,200,000 / $1,300,000
Debt-to-Equity Ratio ≈ 0.9231

71. Answer: C. Receipt of interest income. Receipt of interest income is considered a cash inflow from operating activities. Operating activities involve cash flows directly related to the core operations of the business, such as revenue generation, collection of receivables, and payment of operating expenses. Interest income received is a result of the company's operating activities, and it represents a cash inflow.

72. Answer: B. Investing activities. The investing activities section of the cash flow statement includes cash flows related to the purchase and sale of long-term assets, such as property, plant, and equipment, and investments in other companies. This section reflects the cash flows associated with investments made by the company to expand or maintain its asset base.
73. Answer: D. Cash flow coverage ratio. The cash flow coverage ratio measures a company's ability to generate sufficient cash flow to cover its debt obligations. It is calculated by dividing the operating cash flow by the total debt. This ratio provides an indication of the company's ability to meet its interest and principal payments using its cash flow from operations.
74. Answer: B. $570,000. To calculate the company's cash flow from operating activities using the indirect method, we start with net income and make adjustments for non-cash expenses and changes in working capital.
Net income: $500,000
Add: Depreciation expense: $100,000
Operating income: $600,000
Adjustments for changes in working capital:
Increase in accounts receivable: $50,000 (subtract)
Increase in accounts payable: $20,000 (add)
Cash flow from operating activities: $600,000 - $50,000 + $20,000 = $570,000
75. Answer: B. $1.00. The dividend per share can be calculated using the dividend payout ratio and the earnings per share.
Dividend per share = Dividend Payout Ratio x Earnings per Share
Dividend per share = 40% x $2.50 = $1.00
Therefore, the correct answer is B. $1.00.
76. Answer: C. $3,000,000. The debt-to-equity ratio is calculated by dividing total debt by total equity. Rearranging the formula, we can calculate total debt as:
Total Debt = Debt-to-Equity Ratio x Total Equity
Total Debt = 0.8 x $2,500,000 = $2,000,000
To calculate total assets, we add the total debt to the total equity:

Total Assets = Total Debt + Total Equity
Total Assets = $2,000,000 + $2,500,000 = $3,000,000
77. Answer: C. Higher than industry average. The company's return on assets (ROA) can be calculated as follows:
ROA = Net Profit / Total Assets
ROA = $500,000 / $5,000,000
ROA = 0.10 or 10%
The company's ROA is 10%. To compare it to the industry average, we calculate the industry's ROA:
Industry ROA = Net Profit / Average Total Assets
Industry ROA = $500,000 / $10,000,000
Industry ROA = 0.05 or 5%
Since the company's ROA (10%) is higher than the industry average ROA (5%), it indicates that the company is more efficient in generating profits from its assets compared to the industry.
78. Answer: A. LIFO (Last In, First Out). Under IFRS, the LIFO method is not permitted for inventory valuation. It is allowed under U.S. Generally Accepted Accounting Principles (GAAP).
79. Answer: B. Sales Revenue by Average Inventory. The inventory turnover ratio is calculated by dividing sales revenue by average inventory. It measures how many times a company sells and replaces its inventory within a given period.
80. Answer: D. Net income will be higher compared to LIFO. In a period of rising prices, FIFO assumes that the earliest purchased or produced items are sold first, resulting in a lower cost of goods sold (COGS) compared to the LIFO (Last In, First Out) method. Since COGS is lower, the gross profit and net income will be higher under FIFO.
81. Answer: D. 3.2.
Average Inventory = (Beginning Inventory + Ending Inventory) / 2
Average Inventory = ($100,000 + $150,000) / 2
Average Inventory = $125,000
Inventory Turnover Ratio = Sales / Average Inventory
Inventory Turnover Ratio = $400,000 / $125,000
Inventory Turnover Ratio = 3.2

82. Answer: C. Patents. Patents are examples of intangible long-lived assets. Tangible long-lived assets include buildings, machinery and equipment, and land.
83. Answer: A. $33,333.
    Under the straight-line amortization method, the annual amortization expense for intangible assets is calculated by dividing the cost of the asset by its remaining legal life.
    Amortization Expense = Cost of Asset / Remaining Legal Life
    Amortization Expense = $500,000 / 10
    Amortization Expense = $50,000 per year
    Therefore, the correct answer is A. $33,333 (annual amortization expense).
84. Answer: B. $37,500.
    Under the double-declining balance method, the annual depreciation expense is calculated by multiplying the asset's net book value (cost - accumulated depreciation) by the depreciation rate, which is twice the straight-line rate. The depreciation rate is calculated as 1 / useful life * 2.
    Depreciation Rate = (1 / Useful Life) * 2
    Depreciation Rate = (1 / 8) * 2 = 0.25
    Year 1 Depreciation expense = Net Book Value * Depreciation Rate
    Year 1 Depreciation expense = $200,000 * 0.25 = $50,000
    Year 2 Depreciation Expense = Net Book Value x Depreciation Rate
    Year 2 Depreciation Expense = $150,000 x 0.25 = $37,500
85. Answer: B. Double-declining balance method. The double-declining balance method results in a higher depreciation expense in the earlier years of an asset's life. It applies a higher depreciation rate to the asset's net book value, which declines over time.
86. Answer: A. Deferred tax liabilities result in an increase in future tax payments. Deferred tax liabilities arise when tax expenses are lower than tax payments made in the current period. They represent the future tax obligations that will arise when temporary differences reverse and taxable income is greater than book income. Deferred tax liabilities result in an increase in future tax payments.

87. Answer: B. The deferred tax asset and deferred tax liability should be reported separately on the balance sheet.
According to accounting standards, deferred tax assets and deferred tax liabilities should be presented separately on the balance sheet. They represent different tax consequences associated with temporary differences between book and tax accounting. Offsetting these items against each other is not allowed.
88. Answer: A. $30,000.
The semi-annual interest payment associated with a bond can be calculated by multiplying the bond's face value (principal) by half of the annual coupon rate.
Semi-annual Interest Payment = Bond Face Value x (Coupon Rate / 2)
Semi-annual Interest Payment = $1,000,000 x (0.06 / 2)
Semi-annual Interest Payment = $1,000,000 x 0.03
Semi-annual Interest Payment = $30,000
89. Answer: C. Higher accruals quality. Higher accruals quality is typically associated with higher financial reporting quality. Accruals are adjustments made to financial statements to recognize revenues and expenses that have been earned or incurred but have not yet been received or paid in cash. Higher accruals quality means that accruals are less likely to be manipulated or misstated, resulting in more reliable and accurate financial reporting.
90. Answer: A. ABC Company has a more favorable liquidity position than XYZ Company. The current ratio is calculated by dividing current assets by current liabilities. It measures a company's ability to meet short-term obligations using its short-term assets. If ABC Company has a higher current ratio compared to XYZ Company, it indicates that ABC Company has more current assets relative to its current liabilities. This implies that ABC Company is better positioned to meet its short-term obligations and has a more favorable liquidity position.

Session 2
90 Questions

1. Which of the following is a characteristic of a limited liability company (LLC)?

A) Owners have unlimited personal liability for the company's debts.
B) Ownership interests can be freely transferred without restrictions.
C) It must have a board of directors to oversee its operations.
D) It provides pass-through taxation.

2. Which of the following statements accurately describes the role of the board of directors in corporate governance?

A) The board of directors is responsible for day-to-day operational decisions.
B) The board of directors is accountable to shareholders and oversees the company's management.
C) The board of directors primarily focuses on maximizing short-term profits for the company.
D) The board of directors is not involved in setting the strategic direction of the company.

3. Which of the following is an example of an environmental consideration under the ESG framework?

A) Labor practices and employee relations.
B) Diversity and inclusion in the workplace.
C) Energy consumption and greenhouse gas emissions.
D) Community involvement and philanthropy.

4. Which of the following risks is associated with changes in government regulations or policies that impact a company's operations?

A) Market risk

B) Political risk
C) Credit risk
D) Liquidity risk

5. A company is considering an investment project that requires an initial outlay of $500,000. The project is expected to generate annual cash inflows of $150,000 for five years. The company's required rate of return for similar projects is 10%. What is the project's net present value (NPV) rounded to the nearest dollar?

A) $465,691
B) $750,000
C) $25,000
D) $68,618

6. A company is evaluating two mutually exclusive investment projects, Project A and Project B. The company's required rate of return is 12%. The details of the projects are as follows:

Project A: Initial outlay = $500,000, Annual cash inflows = $150,000 for 4 years
Project B: Initial outlay = $400,000, Annual cash inflows = $120,000 for 5 years
Based on the net present value (NPV) method, which project should the company choose?
A) Project A
B) Project B
C) Both projects are acceptable
D) Neither project is acceptable

7. Which of the following techniques focuses on the calculation of a project's net present value (NPV)?

A) Payback period
B) Internal rate of return (IRR)
C) Accounting rate of return (ARR)
D) Profitability index (PI)

8. A company has the following information for the year:

Current assets: $500,000
Current liabilities: $300,000
Sales revenue: $1,000,000
Cost of goods sold: $600,000
Accounts receivable turnover: 8 times
Inventory turnover: 6 times
What is the company's average collection period for accounts receivable?
A) 45 days
B) 60 days
C) 75 days
D) 90 days

9. A company has the following financial information:

Current assets: $800,000
Current liabilities: $400,000
Cash and cash equivalents: $100,000
Accounts receivable: $200,000
Inventory: $300,000
What is the company's quick ratio?
A) 0.50
B) 0.75
C) 1.00
D) 1.25

10. A company has the following capital structure:

Debt: $2,000,000
Equity: $4,000,000
Weighted average cost of debt: 8%
Weighted average cost of equity: 12%
Tax rate: 25%
What is the company's weighted average cost of capital (WACC)?
A) 9%
B) 10%
C) 11%

D) 12%

11. Which of the following factors is considered when calculating the weighted average cost of capital (WACC)?

A) Dividend yield
B) Return on investment
C) Cost of debt
D) Market capitalization

12. Which of the following statements accurately describes the concept of working capital?

A) Working capital represents the long-term financing obtained by a company to support its ongoing operations.
B) Working capital refers to the excess cash a company holds in its reserves.
C) Working capital measures a company's ability to meet its short-term obligations.
D) Working capital represents the value of a company's fixed assets.

13. Which of the following factors can affect a company's equity beta?

A) The company's level of debt
B) The company's dividend payout ratio
C) The company's accounts receivable turnover
D) The company's industry risk

14. Which of the following factors is typically considered when determining a company's optimal capital structure?

A) The company's industry risk
B) The company's historical stock performance
C) The company's board of directors' preferences
D) The company's revenue growth rate

15. Which of the following is a characteristic of financial leverage in a company's capital structure?

A) It increases the company's profitability.
B) It increases the company's operational risk.
C) It decreases the company's liquidity.
D) It decreases the company's cost of debt.

16. Which of the following measures of leverage indicates the proportion of a company's total assets that is financed by its equity shareholders?

A) Debt-to-Equity Ratio
B) Equity Multiplier
C) Total Debt Ratio
D) Financial Leverage Ratio

17. A company has fixed costs of $100,000, variable costs per unit of $10, and a selling price per unit of $20. What is the breakeven quantity of sales for this company?

A) 5,000 units
B) 10,000 units
C) 15,000 units
D) 20,000 units

18. Company A has fixed costs of $50,000, variable costs per unit of $20, and a selling price per unit of $50. Company B has fixed costs of $100,000, variable costs per unit of $10, and a selling price per unit of $30. Which company has a higher degree of operating leverage?

A) Company A
B) Company B
C) Both companies have the same degree of operating leverage.
D) It cannot be determined based on the given information.

19. Which of the following statements accurately describes the concept of diversification in portfolio management?

A) Diversification reduces the overall risk of a portfolio by investing in multiple securities that are highly correlated.

B) Diversification eliminates the potential for losses in a portfolio by investing in securities from different asset classes.
C) Diversification aims to reduce the risk of a portfolio by investing in securities that move in the same direction.
D) Diversification reduces the risk of a portfolio by investing in securities that have low or negative correlations.

20. Which of the following best describes systematic risk in portfolio management?

A) Systematic risk is the risk associated with an individual security or investment.
B) Systematic risk is the risk that can be eliminated through diversification.
C) Systematic risk is the risk that affects the overall market or a specific sector.
D) Systematic risk is the risk that can be reduced through active portfolio management.

21. An investor has a portfolio consisting of two assets: Asset A and Asset B. Asset A has a weight of 60% in the portfolio and an expected return of 10%. Asset B has a weight of 40% in the portfolio and an expected return of 8%. The correlation between the two assets is 0.6. What is the expected return of the portfolio?

A) 8.8%
B) 9.2%
C) 9.6%
D) 10.4%

22. An investor has a portfolio with two assets: Asset X and Asset Y. Asset X has a weight of 40% and a standard deviation of 15%. Asset Y has a weight of 60% and a standard deviation of 10%. The correlation between the two assets is 0.6. What is the portfolio's overall standard deviation?

A) 9.17%

B) 10.17%
C) 11.17%
D) 12.17%

23. An investor is evaluating two portfolios: Portfolio A and Portfolio B. Portfolio A has an expected return of 12% and a standard deviation of 15%. Portfolio B has an expected return of 10% and a standard deviation of 10%. Which portfolio would be preferred by an investor who is risk-averse and focuses solely on maximizing return per unit of risk?

A) Portfolio A
B) Portfolio B
C) Both portfolios are equally preferred

24. An investor collects the following data:

Risk-free rate of return: 4%
Expected market return: 12%
Standard deviation of market returns: 20%
The investor wants to determine the expected return of a portfolio on the capital market line with a standard deviation of returns of 15%. Which of the following is the closest estimate for the expected return?
Options:
A) 6%
B) 8%
C) 10%
D) 12%

25. An individual investor is in the process of creating an Investment Policy Statement (IPS). Which of the following components is typically included in an IPS?

A) Current market conditions analysis
B) Stock selection strategies
C) Portfolio performance evaluation
D) Risk tolerance assessment

26. A well-designed risk management framework:

A) Involves a systematic approach and provides guidance for conducting risk management activities.
B) Emphasizes the importance of minimizing financial losses rather than solely focusing on policy and process development.
C) Is a structured process that addresses key factors common to various organizations.

27. Which of the following behavioral biases refers to the tendency of individuals to hold onto losing investments and sell winning investments too quickly?

Options:
A) Confirmation bias
B) Loss aversion bias
C) Overconfidence bias
D) Gambler's fallacy bias

28. A technical analyst is examining the price chart of a stock and notices a pattern where the price has been consistently moving up, followed by a period of consolidation, and then a breakout to the upside. This pattern is most likely indicative of:

A) Bullish divergence
B) Bearish divergence
C) Reversal pattern
D) Continuation pattern

29. A technical analyst is examining a price chart and notices a pattern where the price of a stock forms a series of higher highs and higher lows. This pattern is most commonly associated with:

A) Bearish trend
B) Bullish trend
C) Reversal pattern
D) Trading range

30. Which of the following technologies has the potential to revolutionize the investment management industry by automating portfolio construction and trading decisions based on pre-defined rules and algorithms?

A) Blockchain technology
B) Artificial intelligence (AI)
C) Robo-advisors
D) Cryptocurrency

31. Which of the following market structures is characterized by a large number of buyers and sellers, homogeneous products, perfect information, and no barriers to entry or exit?

A) Oligopoly
B) Monopoly
C) Perfect competition
D) Monopolistic competition

32. In a specific market, there are five firms with market shares as follows: Firm A has a market share of 40%, Firm B has a market share of 25%, Firm C has a market share of 20%, Firm D has a market share of 10%, and Firm E has a market share of 5%. What is the Herfindahl-Hirschman Index (HHI) for this market?

A) 2,600
B) 2,550
C) 1,000
D) 2,650

33. In a perfectly competitive market, the current market price for a product is $10. Firm X is producing and selling 100 units of the product at this price. If Firm X decides to increase its production to 150 units, what is likely to happen to the market price?

A) The market price will increase.
B) The market price will decrease.

C) The market price will remain the same.

34. In an oligopoly market, if one of the dominant firms reduces its price significantly, what is likely to happen to the other firms in the market?

A) They will increase their prices.
B) They will decrease their prices.
C) They will keep their prices unchanged.

35. Which of the following statements best describes a market-weighted index?

A) It assigns equal weights to each security in the index.
B) It assigns weights to securities based on their market capitalizations.
C) It assigns weights to securities based on their share price.
D) It assigns weights to securities based on their credit ratings.

36. Which of the following indexes is considered a broad-based market index?

A) S&P 500
B) Dow Jones Industrial Average (DJIA)
C) NASDAQ Composite Index
D) Russell 2000

37. A float-adjusted market-capitalization weighted index:

A) Gives higher weightage to stocks with larger market capitalizations.
B) Adjusts stock weights based on the number of shares outstanding.
C) Includes all stocks in proportion to their market capitalizations.
D) Assigns equal weights to all stocks in the index.

38. Which form of market efficiency suggests that it is impossible to consistently achieve above-average returns by analyzing historical price and trading volume data?

A) Weak form efficiency
B) Semi-strong form efficiency
C) Strong form efficiency
D) Efficient market hypothesis

39. Which of the following is a key implication of the efficient market hypothesis (EMH)?

A) Active management consistently outperforms passive management strategies.
B) Market prices reflect all available public information.
C) It is possible to consistently predict future stock prices based on historical trends.
D) Market participants are irrational and make systematic errors.

40. Which of the following statements regarding market anomalies is true?

A) Market anomalies are consistent with the efficient market hypothesis (EMH).
B) Market anomalies are persistent patterns that can be exploited to consistently generate excess returns.
C) Market anomalies occur randomly and cannot be explained by any underlying factors.
D) Market anomalies only exist in less developed or emerging markets.

41. Which of the following factors may affect the price of common equity securities in the secondary market?

A) The company's financial performance and earnings.
B) Macroeconomic factors such as interest rates and inflation.
C) Investor sentiment and market psychology.
D) All of the above.

42. Which of the following statements accurately describes depository receipts?

A) Global Depository Receipts (GDRs) are only available to institutional investors and not retail investors.
B) Depository receipts allow investors to directly purchase shares of a company in their local currency.
C) American Depository Receipts (ADRs) are issued in the United States and represent ownership in a foreign company.

43. When conducting industry analysis, which of the following factors is considered a macroeconomic factor?

A) Competitive landscape
B) Technological advancements
C) Government regulations
D) Interest rates

44. Which of the following is an example of a primary source of industry data?

A) Industry reports published by research firms
B) Financial statements of individual companies
C) Interviews with industry experts
D) News articles discussing industry trends

45. When analyzing a company's competitive advantage, which of the following frameworks assesses the company's ability to maintain a sustainable competitive position?

A) SWOT analysis
B) Porter's Five Forces model
C) Value chain analysis

46. A company is expected to pay a dividend of $2.50 per share next year. The dividend is expected to grow at a constant rate of 5% per year. If the required rate of return is 10%, what is the estimated intrinsic value of the stock using the dividend discount model (DDM)?

A) $23.81
B) $25.00

C) $50.00
D) $52.50

47. Which of the following factors affects the price-earnings (P/E) ratio of a company?

A) Dividend yield
B) Earnings growth rate
C) Risk-free rate
D) Market capitalization

48. Which of the following valuation multiples is most appropriate to use when valuing a company in a mature industry with stable cash flows?

A) Price/Book Value (P/B) ratio
B) Price/Earnings (P/E) ratio
C) Price/Sales (P/S) ratio
D) Price/Cash Flow (P/CF) ratio

49. A company has reported earnings per share (EPS) of $2.50. The company's historical P/E ratio is 15. Based on the industry average P/E ratio of 20, what is the estimated value of the company's stock?

A) $25.00
B) $30.00
C) $37.50
D) $50.00

50. A company has reported free cash flows of $10 million for the past three years. The weighted average cost of capital (WACC) is 8%. If the company is expected to generate free cash flows of $12 million in the coming year, what is the estimated value of the company using the discounted cash flow (DCF) method?

A) $11.11 million
B) $41.11 million

C) $42 million

51. A bond with a face value of $1,000 has a coupon rate of 5% and pays interest semi-annually. The bond matures in 5 years. If the required yield is 6%, what is the approximate present value of the bond?

A) $957
B) $938
C) $925
D) $1,000

52. A zero-coupon bond has a face value of $1,000 and matures in 3 years. The current market price of the bond is $800. What is the yield to maturity (YTM) of the bond?

A) 4.53%
B) 5.00%
C) 6.25%
D) 7.72%

53. Which of the following statements about the primary market for bonds is true?

A) The primary market refers to the market where bonds are traded after their initial issuance.
B) The primary market is less regulated compared to the secondary market.
C) The primary market facilitates the issuance of new bonds by borrowers to raise capital.

54. Which of the following statements about Eurobonds is correct?

A) Eurobonds are issued by European Union (EU) member countries to finance their budget deficits.
B) Eurobonds are denominated in euros and can only be issued by European companies.

C) Eurobonds are subject to the regulations and oversight of a single European regulatory authority.
D) Eurobonds are typically issued in multiple currencies and can be issued by entities outside of Europe.

55. A bond with a face value of $1,000, a coupon rate of 6%, and a maturity of 10 years has a yield to maturity (YTM) of 8%. What is the bond's current yield?

A) 5%
B) 6%
C) 7%
D) 8%

56. A bond has a yield to maturity (YTM) of 6%, a coupon rate of 5%, and a maturity of 7 years. Which of the following statements is correct regarding the bond's price sensitivity to changes in market interest rates?

A) The bond's price will increase if market interest rates rise.
B) The bond's price will decrease if market interest rates rise.
C) The bond's price will remain unchanged regardless of changes in market interest rates.
D) The bond's price sensitivity cannot be determined without additional information.

57. Which of the following bonds is likely to have the highest duration?

A) A bond with a 2% coupon rate and 5 years to maturity.
B) A bond with a 4% coupon rate and 5 years to maturity.
C) A bond with a 2% coupon rate and 10 years to maturity.
D) A bond with a 4% coupon rate and 10 years to maturity.

58. Which of the following factors is least likely to affect the yield spread of a corporate bond over a comparable government bond?

A) Credit risk

B) Market liquidity
C) Macroeconomic conditions
D) Coupon rate

> 59. A bond has a face value of $1,000, a coupon rate of 7% paid semi-annually, and a yield to maturity (YTM) of 6%. The bond has 10 years remaining until maturity. Calculate the approximate price of the bond.

A) $1,068.23
B) $1,074.39
C) $1,050.45
D) $983.74

> 60. An asset-backed security (ABS) is collateralized by a pool of residential mortgage loans. Which of the following is true regarding the prepayment risk associated with this ABS?

A) Prepayment risk is higher when interest rates decrease.
B) Prepayment risk is higher when interest rates increase.
C) Prepayment risk is not influenced by changes in interest rates.

> 61. Which of the following statements regarding asset-backed securities (ABS) is true?

A) ABS are typically issued by governments to fund public infrastructure projects.
B) ABS have higher credit risk compared to corporate bonds.
C) ABS provide a fixed interest rate to investors.
D) ABS are not subject to prepayment risk.

> 62. When the yield curve is upward-sloping, which of the following statements is true?

A) Long-term bonds have higher yield to maturity than short-term bonds.
B) Short-term bonds have higher yield to maturity than long-term bonds.
C) The term structure of interest rates is flat.

D) Treasury bonds have higher yield to maturity than corporate bonds.

63. Which of the following factors is least likely to affect the credit spread of a corporate bond?

A) Changes in market interest rates.
B) Investor demand for corporate bonds.
C) The company's credit rating.
D) Macroeconomic factors.

64. Which of the following risks is most likely to affect the value of a callable bond?

A) Credit risk.
B) Interest rate risk.
C) Reinvestment risk.
D) Liquidity risk.

65. A bond has a face value of $1,000, a coupon rate of 6% per annum paid annually, and a yield to maturity of 7% per annum. The bond has five years remaining until maturity. What is the Macaulay duration of the bond?

A) 3.50 years
B) 4.25 years
C) 4.45 years
D) 5.00 years

66. The best measure for calculating the weighted average of the time to receipt of a bond's promised future payments is:

A) Effective duration.
B) Macaulay duration.
C) Modified duration.

67. Company XYZ has a current ratio of 1.5, a quick ratio of 1, and a debt-to-equity ratio of 0.8. Which of the following

statements is most accurate regarding the company's liquidity and financial risk?

A) The company has high liquidity and low financial risk.
B) The company has low liquidity and high financial risk.
C) The company has high liquidity but moderate financial risk.
D) The company has low liquidity but low financial risk.

68. Which of the following factors is NOT typically considered when assessing the creditworthiness of a corporate bond issuer?

A) Financial ratios and credit metrics.
B) Industry and market conditions.
C) Management team and corporate governance.
D) Historical stock price performance.

69. Company ABC has recently been downgraded by a credit rating agency. Which of the following statements is most accurate regarding the implications of this downgrade?

A) The company's borrowing costs are likely to decrease.
B) The company's creditworthiness has improved.
C) The company's ability to access capital markets may be negatively impacted.
D) The company's profitability is expected to increase.

70. An investor enters into a futures contract to sell 100 shares of Company XYZ at a price of $50 per share. If the price of Company XYZ stock increases to $60 per share at time of maturity, what will be the impact on the investor's position?

A) The investor will incur a loss.
B) The investor will earn a profit.
C) The investor's position will remain unchanged.
D) The impact cannot be determined without additional information.

71. An investor enters into a long position in a call option on Stock ABC with a strike price of $100 and a premium of $5.

If the price of Stock ABC increases to $120 at expiration, what will be the investor's profit or loss?

A) $15 profit
B) $20 profit
C) $25 profit
D) $20 loss

72. A company enters into a forward contract to purchase 1,000 barrels of crude oil at a price of $70 per barrel. At the expiration of the contract, the spot price of crude oil is $80 per barrel. What will be the company's gain or loss from the forward contract?

A) $10,000 gain
B) $10,000 loss
C) $0 gain or loss
D) $5,000 gain

73. Which of the following statements regarding the benefits and risks of derivatives is true?

A) Derivatives provide a guaranteed return and eliminate all investment risk.
B) Derivatives offer leverage and the potential for amplified gains or losses.
C) Derivatives have no impact on market liquidity.
D) Derivatives are primarily used to reduce transaction costs.

74. An investor notices that the price of a stock index futures contract is higher than the corresponding stock index. Which of the following actions is most likely to be profitable based on this observation?

A) Buy the stock index futures contract and sell short the corresponding stock index.
B) Sell the stock index futures contract and buy the corresponding stock index.

C) Buy the stock index futures contract and buy the corresponding stock index.
D) Sell the stock index futures contract and sell short the corresponding stock index.
A) Buy the stock index futures contract and sell short the corresponding stock index.

75. Which of the following factors influences the price of a call option on a stock?

A) The stock's volatility.
B) The stock's dividend yield.
C) The risk-free interest rate.
D) All of the above.

76. Which scenario is most likely to result in a difference in pricing between forwards and futures?

A) When interest rates show no volatility.
B) When there is a negative correlation between futures prices and interest rates.
C) When there is no correlation between futures prices and interest rates.

77. A company enters into an interest rate swap where it pays a fixed rate and receives a floating rate based on LIBOR. The notional amount of the swap is $20 million. If the floating rate is reset annually and the fixed rate for the upcoming year is higher than the expected floating rate, how will this affect the net payment made or received by the company?

A) The company will make a net payment.
B) The company will receive a net payment.
C) The net payment will remain unchanged.

78. An investor purchases a call option on a stock with a strike price of $50 and a premium of $3. The stock is currently trading at $55. If the investor exercises the call option when

the stock price is $60, what is the intrinsic value and time value of the option at that point?

A) Intrinsic value: $5, Time value: $2
B) Intrinsic value: $10, Time value: $0
C) Intrinsic value: $5, Time value: $3
D) Intrinsic value: $10, Time value: $3

79. An investor wants to replicate the payoff of a call option using put options and other securities. Which of the following combinations achieves this replication strategy?

A) Buy a put option and buy the underlying asset.
B) Sell a put option and sell the underlying asset.
C) Buy a put option and sell the underlying asset.
D) Sell a put option and buy the underlying asset.

80. You are valuing a European call option using a one-period binomial model. The stock price is currently $50, the exercise price is $55, the risk-free rate is 5%, and the probability of an up move in the stock price is 0.6. What is the value of the call option?

A) $14.29
B) $15.00
C) $17.50
D) $20.00

81. Which of the following alternative investments is typically characterized by a fixed term, illiquidity, and a focus on capital preservation?

A) Venture capital
B) Real estate
C) Hedge funds
D) Private equity

82. Which compensation structure is commonly associated with private equity investments?

A) Management fees and carried interest
B) Performance fees
C) Expense ratio

83. An investor purchased a hedge fund investment with a total capital commitment of $500,000. The investment has a management fee of 2% per year and a performance fee of 20% of the profits. In the first year, the fund generated a return of 12%. Calculate the total fees paid by the investor for the first year.

A) $20,000
B) $22,000
C) $24,000
D) $32,000

84. Which of the following alternative investments is typically associated with a lock-up period?

A) Publicly traded stocks
B) Treasury bonds
C) Hedge funds
D) Real estate investment trusts (REITs)

85. A private equity investment returned 20% per year over a holding period of 5 years. The investment had an initial capital commitment of $1,000,000. Calculate the total investment value at the end of the holding period.

A) $1,244,860
B) $1,400,000
C) $1,488,320
D) $1,580,220

86. Which of the following is a characteristic of private equity investments?

A) High liquidity
B) Publicly traded

C) Short-term investment horizon
D) Active involvement in portfolio companies

87. Which of the following is NOT a typical risk associated with infrastructure investments?

A) Regulatory risk
B) Construction risk
C) Market risk
D) Managerial risk

88. Which of the following asset classes is typically associated with inflation hedging and stable cash flow generation?

A) Hedge funds
B) Infrastructure
C) Natural resources
D) Real estate

89. Which of the following characteristics is typically associated with hedge funds using a global macro strategy?

A) High portfolio turnover
B) Focus on short-term trading
C) Emphasis on bottom-up stock picking
D) Use of macroeconomic analysis and trends

90. Which of the following alternative investments is typically characterized by longer lock-up periods and limited liquidity?

A) Private equity
B) Hedge funds
C) Infrastructure funds
D) Natural resources investments

Session 2 Answers

Answers:

1. Answer: D) It provides pass-through taxation. A characteristic of a limited liability company (LLC) is that it provides pass-through taxation. This means that the LLC itself is not taxed at the entity level. Instead, the profits and losses of the LLC pass through to the individual owners, who report them on their personal tax returns. This avoids the issue of double taxation that is typically associated with corporations.
2. Answer: B) The board of directors is accountable to shareholders and oversees the company's management. The board of directors plays a crucial role in corporate governance by representing the interests of shareholders and overseeing the company's management. They are responsible for making strategic decisions, setting corporate objectives, and monitoring the company's performance. The board acts

as a fiduciary to shareholders, ensuring that management acts in the best interests of the company and its stakeholders.
3. Answer: C) Energy consumption and greenhouse gas emissions. Environmental considerations refer to factors related to the impact of a company's operations on the environment. This includes aspects such as energy consumption, greenhouse gas emissions, waste management, pollution control, and natural resource conservation. These factors are essential components of the ESG (Environmental, Social, and Governance) framework, which evaluates a company's sustainability and responsible business practices.
4. Answer: B) Political risk. Political risk is associated with changes in government regulations or policies that can significantly impact a company's operations and profitability. This risk arises from uncertainties related to political events, such as changes in government, new regulations, trade restrictions, or geopolitical tensions. Political risk can lead to adverse effects on a company's financial performance, including disruptions in supply chains, changes in tax policies, or limitations on market access.
5. Answer: D) $68,618. To calculate the net present value (NPV) of the investment project, we need to discount the cash inflows at the company's required rate of return. Here's the calculation:
Year 1: $150,000 / (1 + 0.10)^1 = $136,364
Year 2: $150,000 / (1 + 0.10)^2 = $123,967
Year 3: $150,000 / (1 + 0.10)^3 = $112,697
Year 4: $150,000 / (1 + 0.10)^4 = $102,452
Year 5: $150,000 / (1 + 0.10)^5 = $93,138
Now, we calculate the NPV by subtracting the initial outlay from the discounted cash inflows:
NPV = -$500,000 + $136,364 + $123,967 + $112,697 + $102,452 + $93,138
NPV = $68,618
6. Answer: B) Project B. To determine the project to choose based on the net present value (NPV) method, we need to calculate the NPV for each project. Using the required rate of return of 12%, let's calculate the NPV for each project:
For Project A:

$NPV\_A = -\$500,000 + \$150,000 / (1 + 0.12)^{\wedge}1 + \$150,000 / (1 + 0.12)^{\wedge}2 + \$150,000 / (1 + 0.12)^{\wedge}3 + \$150,000 / (1 + 0.12)^{\wedge}4$

$NPV\_A = -\$500,000 + \$133,929 + \$119,628 + \$106,562 + \$95,066$

$NPV\_A = -\$44,815$

For Project B:

$NPV\_B = -\$400,000 + \$120,000 / (1 + 0.12)^{\wedge}1 + \$120,000 / (1 + 0.12)^{\wedge}2 + \$120,000 / (1 + 0.12)^{\wedge}3 + \$120,000 / (1 + 0.12)^{\wedge}4 + \$120,000 / (1 + 0.12)^{\wedge}5$

$NPV\_B = -\$400,000 + \$107,143 + \$95,578 + \$85,310 + \$76,206 + \$68,027$

$NPV\_B = \$32,264$

Comparing the NPVs, we find that Project A has an NPV of -$44,815, while Project B has an NPV of $32,264. Since the NPV of Project B is positive and higher than the NPV of Project A, the company should choose Project B.

7. Answer: B) Internal rate of return (IRR). The internal rate of return (IRR) is a capital investment technique that focuses on calculating a project's net present value (NPV). The IRR is the discount rate at which the present value of cash inflows equals the present value of cash outflows. By comparing the IRR to the required rate of return, investors can determine the feasibility and attractiveness of an investment project.

8. Answer: A) 45 days. To calculate the average collection period for accounts receivable, we use the formula:
Average Collection Period = 365 days / Accounts Receivable Turnover
In this case, the accounts receivable turnover is 8 times. Therefore:
Average Collection Period = 365 days / 8 = 45.625 days

9. Answer: B) 0.75. The quick ratio, also known as the acid-test ratio, measures a company's ability to meet its short-term obligations using its most liquid assets. It is calculated as follows:
Quick Ratio = (Cash and Cash Equivalents + Accounts Receivable) / Current Liabilities

In this case, the cash and cash equivalents are $100,000, and the accounts receivable are $200,000. The current liabilities are $400,000.
Quick Ratio = ($100,000 + $200,000) / $400,000
Quick Ratio = $300,000 / $400,000
Quick Ratio = 0.75

10. Answer: B) 10%. The weighted average cost of capital (WACC) is the average rate of return required by both debt and equity investors. It is calculated as follows:
Weight of Debt = (Debt / (Debt + Equity)) × (1 - Tax rate)
Weight of Debt = ($2,000,000 / ($2,000,000 + $4,000,000)) × (1 - 0.25) = 0.3333 × 0.75 = 0.249975
Weight of Equity = ($4,000,000 / ($2,000,000 + $4,000,000)) = 0.6667
Now, we can calculate the WACC:
WACC = (Weight of Debt × Cost of Debt) + (Weight of Equity × Cost of Equity)
WACC = (0.249975 × 8%) + (0.6667 × 12%) = 0.019998 + 0.080004 = 0.099997
Since the WACC is typically expressed as a percentage, we multiply by 100:
WACC = 0.099997 × 100 = 9.9997%

11. Answer: C) Cost of debt. The weighted average cost of capital (WACC) is a key metric used to evaluate a company's investment opportunities. It represents the average rate of return required by both debt and equity investors. When calculating WACC, several factors are considered, including the cost of debt.

12. Answer: C) Working capital measures a company's ability to meet its short-term obligations. Working capital is a measure of a company's liquidity and its ability to cover its short-term obligations. It represents the difference between current assets and current liabilities. Positive working capital indicates that a company has sufficient resources to meet its short-term debts and operational expenses.

13. Answer: D) The company's industry risk. Equity beta measures the sensitivity of a stock's returns to changes in the overall market. It captures the systematic risk of the stock. While various factors can influence a company's equity beta,

the primary factor is the industry risk in which the company operates.
14. Answer: A) The company's industry risk. Determining a company's optimal capital structure involves assessing various factors to find the right mix of debt and equity financing. However, the primary consideration is typically the company's industry risk.
15. Answer: B) It increases the company's operational risk. Financial leverage refers to the use of debt financing in a company's capital structure. While it can have certain benefits, such as magnifying returns to shareholders, it also introduces additional risks. One of these risks is increased operational risk.
16. Answer: B) Equity Multiplier. The equity multiplier is a measure of leverage that indicates the proportion of a company's total assets that is financed by its equity shareholders. It is calculated as the ratio of total assets to total equity.
17. Answer: B) 10,000 units. To calculate the breakeven quantity of sales, we need to determine the point at which the company's total costs equal its total revenue. This occurs when the contribution margin (selling price per unit minus variable cost per unit) covers the fixed costs.
In this case, the contribution margin per unit is $20 - $10 = $10. The fixed costs are given as $100,000.
Breakeven Quantity of Sales = Fixed Costs / Contribution Margin per Unit
= $100,000 / $10
= 10,000 units
18. Answer: B) Company B.
The degree of operating leverage (DOL) measures the sensitivity of a company's operating income to changes in sales volume. It is calculated as the percentage change in operating income divided by the percentage change in sales.
DOL = (% Change in Operating Income) / (% Change in Sales)
In this case, we are comparing Company A and Company B based on their fixed costs, variable costs per unit, and selling price per unit.

Company A:
Fixed costs = $50,000
Variable costs per unit = $20
Selling price per unit = $50
Company B:
Fixed costs = $100,000
Variable costs per unit = $10
Selling price per unit = $30
To compare the DOL of both companies, we need more information about the sales volume or percentage changes in sales. Since this information is not provided, we cannot determine the exact DOL for each company. However, we can make a general comparison based on the given information.
Company B has higher fixed costs and lower variable costs per unit compared to Company A. This implies that a larger portion of Company B's cost structure consists of fixed costs. Generally, a higher proportion of fixed costs results in a higher degree of operating leverage. Therefore, we can conclude that Company B likely has a higher degree of operating leverage.

19. Answer: D) Diversification reduces the risk of a portfolio by investing in securities that have low or negative correlations. Diversification is a key concept in portfolio management and involves spreading investments across different securities or asset classes to reduce risk. The correct answer is D) Diversification reduces the risk of a portfolio by investing in securities that have low or negative correlations.

20. Answer: C) Systematic risk is the risk that affects the overall market or a specific sector. Systematic risk, also known as market risk or non-diversifiable risk, refers to the risk that affects the entire market or a specific sector. It is beyond the control of an individual investor or company. The correct answer is C) Systematic risk is the risk that affects the overall market or a specific sector.

21. Answer: B) 9.2%. To calculate the expected return of a portfolio, we need to consider the weights and expected returns of the individual assets. The formula for the expected return of a portfolio is:

Expected Return of Portfolio = Weight of Asset A × Expected Return of Asset A + Weight of Asset B × Expected Return of Asset B

Using the formula, we can calculate the expected return of the portfolio as follows:

Expected Return of Portfolio = (0.6 × 0.10) + (0.4 × 0.08)
= 0.06 + 0.032
= 0.092

22. Answer: B) 10.17%. Using the formula for the overall standard deviation of a two-asset portfolio, we can calculate:

Portfolio Standard Deviation = $\sqrt{[(\text{Weight of Asset X})^2 \times (\text{Standard Deviation of Asset X})^2 + (\text{Weight of Asset Y})^2 \times (\text{Standard Deviation of Asset Y})^2 + 2 \times (\text{Weight of Asset X}) \times (\text{Weight of Asset Y}) \times (\text{Standard Deviation of Asset X}) \times (\text{Standard Deviation of Asset Y}) \times (\text{Correlation})]}$

Plugging in the values, we have:

Portfolio Standard Deviation = $\sqrt{[(0.40^2 \times 0.15^2) + (0.60^2 \times 0.10^2) + (2 \times 0.40 \times 0.60 \times 0.15 \times 0.10 \times 0.6)]}$
= $\sqrt{[(0.0036) + (0.0036) + (0.00432)]}$
= $\sqrt{[0.01152]}$
≈ 0.1073
≈ 10.73%

23. Answer: B) Portfolio B. When an investor is risk-averse and focuses solely on maximizing return per unit of risk, they prefer a higher return with lower risk. In this case, Portfolio B has a lower standard deviation (10%) compared to Portfolio A (15%), indicating lower risk. Additionally, Portfolio B still offers a respectable expected return of 10%. Therefore, Portfolio B would be the preferred choice as it provides a higher return per unit of risk.

24. Answer: C) 10%. The capital market line (CML) represents the relationship between expected return and standard deviation for an efficient portfolio. The slope of the CML is the market risk premium, which is calculated as the difference between the expected market return and the risk-free rate. To estimate the expected return on the CML for a portfolio with a standard deviation of returns of 15%, we can use the formula:

Expected Return = Risk-free rate + (Standard deviation of portfolio / Standard deviation of market) * (Expected market return - Risk-free rate)
Plugging in the given values, we have:
Expected Return = 4% + (15% / 20%) * (12% - 4%)
= 4% + (0.75) * (8%)
= 4% + 6%
= 10%

25. Answer: D) Risk tolerance assessment. An Investment Policy Statement (IPS) is a document that outlines an individual's or institution's investment objectives, constraints, and guidelines. It serves as a guide for making investment decisions and provides a framework for managing investments. While all the options listed may be important considerations in the investment process, a risk tolerance assessment is typically a crucial component of an IPS. It helps determine the level of risk an investor is willing and able to take, which in turn influences the asset allocation and investment strategy.

26. Answer: C) Is a structured process that addresses key factors common to various organizations. A robust risk management framework encompasses various essential components, including risk governance, risk infrastructure, policies and procedures, risk monitoring, and integration. These elements are fundamental to effective risk management within an organization. The development of a risk management framework aligns with the definition of risk management provided earlier, as it serves as the foundation, process, and analytical framework necessary to support effective risk management practices.

27. Answer: B) Loss aversion bias. Loss aversion bias refers to the tendency of individuals to strongly prefer avoiding losses rather than acquiring equivalent gains. In the context of investment decisions, this bias manifests as holding onto losing investments for too long in the hopes of recovering losses, while selling winning investments too quickly to secure gains. This behavior can lead to suboptimal investment outcomes and hinder long-term portfolio performance.

28. Answer: D) Continuation pattern. A continuation pattern is a technical analysis pattern that suggests the current trend is likely to continue after a period of consolidation. In this case, the price has been consistently moving up, followed by a period of consolidation, and then a breakout to the upside. This pattern indicates that the upward trend is likely to continue.
29. Answer: B) Bullish trend. When the price of a stock forms a series of higher highs and higher lows, it indicates a bullish trend. A bullish trend suggests that buyers are in control, and the price is likely to continue moving higher.
30. Answer: C) Robo-advisors. Robo-advisors are a type of financial technology (fintech) that use algorithms and automated processes to provide investment advice and manage portfolios for clients. They can automate various aspects of investment management, including portfolio construction, asset allocation, and rebalancing, based on pre-defined rules and algorithms. Robo-advisors aim to provide cost-effective and efficient investment solutions to individual investors.
31. Answer: C) Perfect competition. Perfect competition is a market structure characterized by a large number of buyers and sellers, homogeneous products (where each product is identical to others), perfect information (where all participants have access to the same information), and no barriers to entry or exit. In perfect competition, no single participant has the power to influence prices or market conditions.
32. Answer: D) 2650. To calculate the Herfindahl-Hirschman Index (HHI), we square the market shares of each firm and sum them up.
HHI = $(0.40^2) + (0.25^2) + (0.20^2) + (0.10^2) + (0.05^2)$
= $0.16 + 0.0625 + 0.04 + 0.01 + 0.0025 = 0.265$
Finally, we multiply the result by 10,000 to get the HHI in terms of points.
HHI = $0.265 * 10,000 = 2,650$
33. Answer: C) The market price will remain the same. In a perfectly competitive market, each firm is a price taker, meaning it has no control over the market price. The market

price is determined by the overall supply and demand in the market. When Firm X increases its production from 100 units to 150 units, it will have a marginal impact on the overall market supply, but it is unlikely to significantly affect the market price. Therefore, the market price is expected to remain the same.
34. Answer: B) They will decrease their prices. In an oligopoly market, where a few large firms dominate the industry, firms are interdependent and their actions affect each other. If one dominant firm reduces its price significantly, the other firms are likely to respond by reducing their prices as well to remain competitive. This price competition among the firms is a common characteristic of oligopoly markets, as firms strive to maintain or gain market share.
35. Answer: B) It assigns weights to securities based on their market capitalizations. A market-weighted index, also known as a capitalization-weighted index, assigns weights to securities based on their market capitalizations. Market capitalization is calculated by multiplying the number of outstanding shares of a company by its current market price per share. In a market-weighted index, the weight of each security in the index is proportional to its market capitalization relative to the total market capitalization of all securities in the index.
36. Answer: A) S&P 500. The S&P 500 is considered a broad-based market index. It includes 500 large-cap U.S. companies listed on the New York Stock Exchange (NYSE) and the NASDAQ Stock Market. The index is designed to represent a wide range of industries and sectors in the U.S. equity market, providing a comprehensive view of the overall stock market performance.
37. Answer: B) Adjusts stock weights based on the number of shares outstanding. A float-adjusted market-capitalization weighted index is a type of index that adjusts the weights of stocks based on the number of shares available to the public, also known as the float. The index gives higher weightage to stocks with larger market capitalizations, but it takes into account the portion of shares that are freely available for trading in the market.

38. Answer: A) Weak form efficiency. Weak form efficiency suggests that it is impossible to consistently achieve above-average returns by analyzing historical price and trading volume data alone. This means that all past information, including historical prices, trading volumes, and technical analysis, is already reflected in the current market prices. Therefore, it is not possible to gain an advantage by using this information to make profitable investment decisions.
39. Answer: B) Market prices reflect all available public information. One of the key implications of the efficient market hypothesis (EMH) is that market prices fully reflect all available public information. This means that any new information, such as company announcements, financial reports, or news events, is quickly and accurately incorporated into the market price of a security. As a result, it is difficult to consistently achieve above-average returns by analyzing this publicly available information alone.
40. Answer: C) Market anomalies occur randomly and cannot be explained by any underlying factors. Market anomalies are observed patterns or behaviors in financial markets that cannot be explained by fundamental or rational factors. They occur randomly and represent deviations from the efficient market hypothesis. These anomalies suggest that there may be inefficiencies or biases in the market that allow investors to exploit them and generate abnormal returns.
41. Answer: D) All of the above. Various factors can influence the price of common equity securities in the secondary market. These factors include the company's financial performance and earnings (option A), which directly impact investors' expectations of future profitability. Positive financial results and earnings growth generally tend to increase the demand for the stock, leading to an increase in its price.
42. Answer: C) American Depository Receipts (ADRs) are issued in the United States and represent ownership in a foreign company. Depository receipts are financial instruments that represent ownership in a foreign company but are traded in a different market than the company's home country.

43. Answer: D) Interest rates. When conducting industry analysis, macroeconomic factors refer to broader economic variables that impact multiple industries. Interest rates are one such macroeconomic factor as they influence borrowing costs, investment decisions, and overall economic activity.
44. Answer: B) Financial statements of individual companies. Primary sources of industry data refer to original and firsthand information that comes directly from the source. In the context of industry analysis, financial statements of individual companies are considered primary sources as they provide detailed information about the financial performance and position of companies within the industry.
45. Answer: B) Porter's Five Forces model. Porter's Five Forces model is a framework used to analyze the competitive environment of an industry and assess the company's competitive advantage. It examines five key forces that shape industry competition, including the bargaining power of buyers, bargaining power of suppliers, threat of new entrants, threat of substitute products or services, and intensity of competitive rivalry. By evaluating these forces, the model helps identify the company's position within the industry and its ability to maintain a sustainable competitive advantage.
46. Answer: C) $50.00. The dividend discount model (DDM) is used to estimate the intrinsic value of a stock based on its expected future dividends. The formula for the DDM is: Intrinsic Value = Next Year Dividend / (Required Rate of Return - Dividend Growth Rate). In this case, the dividend is $2.50, the required rate of return is 10%, and the dividend growth rate is 5%. Plugging these values into the formula: Intrinsic Value = $2.50 / (0.10 - 0.05) = $2.50 / 0.05 = $50.00.
47. Answer: B) Earnings growth rate. The price-earnings (P/E) ratio is a valuation ratio that compares a company's stock price to its earnings per share (EPS). The P/E ratio is influenced by various factors, but one of the most significant factors is the earnings growth rate. A higher earnings growth rate is generally associated with a higher P/E ratio, indicating that investors expect higher future earnings from the company.

48. Answer: B) Price/Earnings (P/E) ratio. The P/E ratio is a commonly used valuation multiple that compares a company's stock price to its earnings per share (EPS). It is widely used for valuing companies in various industries, including mature industries with stable cash flows. The P/E ratio reflects the market's assessment of the company's earnings potential and is particularly suitable for companies with predictable and stable earnings.
49. Correct Answer: D) $50.00. To estimate the value of the company's stock, we can multiply the EPS by the industry average P/E ratio. In this case, EPS is $2.50 and the industry average P/E ratio is 20. Estimated Stock Value = EPS x P/E ratio = $2.50 x 20 = $50.00.
50. Correct Answer: B) $41.11 million. To calculate the estimated value of the company using the DCF method, we need to discount the future cash flows to their present value. In this case, the company is expected to generate free cash flows of $12 million in the coming year.
Using a WACC of 8%, we can calculate the present value of this cash flow:
Present Value = Future Cash Flow / (1 + WACC)^n
Present Value = $12 million / (1 + 0.08)^1 = $11.11 million.
Next, we sum up the present values of the past three years' cash flows:
$10 million + $10 million + $10 million = $30 million.
Finally, we add the present value of the coming year's cash flow:
$30 million + $11.11 million = $41.11 million.
51. Answer: A) $957. To calculate the present value of the bond, we need to discount the future cash flows (coupon payments and the face value) to their present value. The bond pays semi-annual coupons, so it will make 10 coupon payments over its 5-year life.
Using the formula for present value of a bond:
Present Value = (Coupon Payment / (1 + Yield/2)^1) + (Coupon Payment / (1 + Yield/2)^2) + ... + (Coupon Payment / (1 + Yield/2)^10) + (Face Value / (1 + Yield/2)^10)
Present Value = (25 / (1 + 0.06/2)^1) + (25 / (1 + 0.06/2)^2) + ... + (25 / (1 + 0.06/2)^10) + (1,000 / (1 + 0.06/2)^10)

Calculating the present value using this formula, we find that the approximate present value of the bond is $957.35, which corresponds to Option A).

52. Answer: D) 7.72%. To calculate the yield to maturity (YTM) of a zero-coupon bond, we can use the following formula:
YTM = (Face Value / Current Market Price)^(1/n) - 1
Substituting the given values:
YTM = ($1,000 / $800)^(1/3) - 1
Calculating the value, we get YTM ≈ 0.0772 or 7.72%, which corresponds to Option D).

53. Answer: C) The primary market facilitates the issuance of new bonds by borrowers to raise capital. The primary market is where new bonds are issued and sold to investors for the first time. In this market, borrowers (such as governments and corporations) raise capital by issuing new debt securities. Institutional and retail investors participate in the primary market to purchase these newly issued bonds. Therefore, option C is the correct answer.

54. Answer: D) Eurobonds are typically issued in multiple currencies and can be issued by entities outside of Europe. Eurobonds are international bonds that are issued in a currency other than the domestic currency of the country where they are issued. They are not limited to being denominated in euros and can be issued in various currencies such as US dollars, Japanese yen, or British pounds. Additionally, Eurobonds are not exclusive to European companies or EU member countries. Entities from any part of the world can issue Eurobonds. While Eurobonds are widely traded in Europe, they are not subject to a single European regulatory authority but rather subject to the regulations of the jurisdictions in which they are issued.

55. Answer: C) 7%. The current yield is calculated by dividing the annual coupon payment by the current market price of the bond. In this case, the annual coupon payment is 6% of the face value, which is $60. Since the bond is trading at a yield to maturity (YTM) of 8%, we can calculate the market price which is $865.80. Therefore, the current yield is $60 / $865.80 = 0.0693. Rounded to the nearest whole number, the current yield is 7%.

56. Answer: B) The bond's price will decrease if market interest rates rise. Bond prices and market interest rates have an inverse relationship. When market interest rates rise, the present value of the bond's future cash flows decreases, resulting in a lower bond price. Conversely, when market interest rates decrease, the present value of the bond's future cash flows increases, leading to a higher bond price. Therefore, the correct statement is that the bond's price will decrease if market interest rates rise.
57. Answer: C) A bond with a 2% coupon rate and 10 years to maturity. Duration is influenced by both the time to maturity and the size of the coupon payments. Generally, the longer the time to maturity and the lower the coupon rate, the higher the duration.
58. Answer: D) Coupon rate. The yield spread of a corporate bond over a comparable government bond is primarily influenced by factors such as credit risk, market liquidity, and macroeconomic conditions. The coupon rate, however, does not directly affect the yield spread. The coupon rate determines the periodic interest payments made by the bond, but it does not have a direct impact on the spread between corporate and government bond yields.
59. Answer: B) $1,074.39.
    We need to calculate the present value of each cash flow using the formula:
    $PV = PMT / (1 + r)^n$
    where PV is the present value, PMT is the cash flow, r is the discount rate, and n is the number of periods.
    For the coupon payments, we have:
    PV of the coupon payments = $(\$35 / (1 + 0.03)^1) + (\$35 / (1 + 0.03)^2) + ... + (\$35 / (1 + 0.03)^{20})$
    For the face value, we have:
    PV of the face value = $(\$1,000 / (1 + 0.03)^{20})$
    Adding up the present values of the coupon payments and the face value gives us the approximate price of the bond. Calculating the above equation, we find the approximate price of the bond to be $1,074.39.
60. Answer: A) Prepayment risk is higher when interest rates decrease. Prepayment risk refers to the risk that borrowers

will repay their loans earlier than expected, which impacts the cash flows of an asset-backed security. When interest rates decrease, borrowers are more likely to refinance their mortgages, leading to higher prepayments. Conversely, when interest rates increase, the incentive for borrowers to refinance diminishes, resulting in lower prepayment rates.

61. Answer: B) ABS have higher credit risk compared to corporate bonds. Asset-backed securities (ABS) are securities that are backed by pools of underlying assets, such as mortgages, auto loans, or credit card receivables. Unlike corporate bonds, which are issued by corporations and backed by their general creditworthiness, ABS rely on the cash flows generated by the underlying assets for repayment. This introduces additional credit risk, as the performance of the underlying assets directly impacts the ability of the ABS to make payments to investors. Therefore, ABS generally have higher credit risk compared to corporate bonds. Options A, C, and D are incorrect as they do not accurately describe ABS characteristics.

62. Answer: A) Long-term bonds have higher yield to maturity than short-term bonds. An upward-sloping yield curve implies that long-term interest rates are higher than short-term interest rates. This means that long-term bonds, which have longer maturities, generally offer higher yields to maturity compared to short-term bonds. Option B is incorrect because short-term bonds have lower yields to maturity in an upward-sloping yield curve environment. Options C and D are unrelated to the shape of the yield curve.

63. Answer: A) Changes in market interest rates. Credit spread refers to the difference in yield between a corporate bond and a risk-free government bond with the same maturity. While changes in market interest rates can influence the price and yield of all bonds, credit spread specifically reflects the credit risk associated with a corporate bond. Factors such as investor demand, the company's credit rating, and macroeconomic conditions are more directly related to credit risk and are more likely to affect the credit spread.

64. Answer: B) Interest rate risk. Interest rate risk refers to the risk of changes in market interest rates affecting the value of

a bond. Callable bonds have an embedded call option that allows the issuer to redeem the bond before its maturity. When interest rates decline, the issuer may exercise the call option and refinance the bond at a lower interest rate, leading to a decrease in the bond's value. Therefore, interest rate risk is the most likely risk to affect the value of a callable bond. Option B is the correct answer.

65. Answer: C) 4.45 years
Present value of the bond = $959.
Macaulay Duration = $[(60 / (1 + 0.07)^1) + (60 / (1 + 0.07)^2) + (60 / (1 + 0.07)^3) + (60 / (1 + 0.07)^4) + (60+1000 / (1 + 0.07)^5)] / 959$
Macaulay Duration ≈ 4.45 years

66. Answer: B) Macaulay duration. Macaulay duration represents the weighted average of the time until the bond's promised payments are received, with the weights assigned based on the proportion of the bond's full price associated with each future payment.

67. Answer: C) The company has high liquidity but moderate financial risk. The current ratio and quick ratio indicate that the company has sufficient current assets to cover its current liabilities, suggesting good liquidity. However, the debt-to-equity ratio of 0.8 indicates that the company has a moderate level of financial risk since it has a relatively high amount of debt compared to its equity.

68. Answer: D) Historical stock price performance. When assessing the creditworthiness of a corporate bond issuer, factors such as financial ratios and credit metrics, industry and market conditions, and management team and corporate governance are commonly considered. However, historical stock price performance is not directly relevant to evaluating creditworthiness as it primarily reflects the equity market's perception and does not directly measure the issuer's ability to fulfill its bond obligations.

69. Answer: C) The company's ability to access capital markets may be negatively impacted. When a company is downgraded by a credit rating agency, it indicates a deterioration in its creditworthiness. This can result in higher borrowing costs as lenders demand a higher yield to

compensate for the increased risk. Additionally, the downgrade may negatively impact the company's reputation and investor confidence, potentially limiting its ability to access capital markets and raise funds through debt issuance or equity offerings. Therefore, option C is the most accurate statement in terms of the implications of the downgrade.

70. Answer: A) The investor will incur a loss. In a futures contract, the investor agrees to sell the underlying asset at a specific price in the future. In this case, the investor has entered into a futures contract to sell 100 shares of Company XYZ at $50 per share. If the price of Company XYZ stock increases to $60 per share, the investor is obligated to sell the shares at $50 per share as per the contract. Therefore, the investor will incur a loss as they could have sold the shares at a higher price in the market. Option A is the correct answer.

71. Answer: A) $15 profit. In a long call option position, the investor has the right to buy the underlying stock at the strike price. If the price of the stock increases to $120 at expiration, the investor can exercise the call option and buy the stock at the strike price of $100. They can then sell the stock in the market for $120, resulting in a profit of $20 per share. Since the option contract represents 1 share, the total profit would be $20. Additionally, the investor paid a premium of $5 to acquire the option initially. Therefore, the total profit from the call option would be $20 - $5 = $15.

72. Answer: A) $10,000 gain. In a forward contract, the parties agree to buy or sell an underlying asset at a predetermined price at a future date. In this case, the company has entered into a forward contract to purchase crude oil at $70 per barrel. At expiration, the spot price is $80 per barrel. Since the company has agreed to buy the oil at $70 per barrel, but the market price is higher at $80 per barrel, the company will realize a gain of $10 per barrel. With a contract size of 1,000 barrels, the total gain from the forward contract will be $10 x 1,000 = $10,000.

73. Answer: B) Derivatives offer leverage and the potential for amplified gains or losses. Derivatives provide leverage, allowing investors to control a larger position with a smaller upfront investment. While this can result in amplified gains,

it also exposes investors to greater losses. Derivatives do not guarantee a return and do not eliminate investment risk. They can have an impact on market liquidity, especially in the case of highly liquid derivative contracts. Finally, while derivatives can help manage transaction costs in certain cases, their primary purpose is not to reduce transaction costs.

74. Answer: A) Buy the stock index futures contract and sell short the corresponding stock index. If the price of the stock index futures contract is higher than the corresponding stock index, it suggests that there is an opportunity for arbitrage. By buying the futures contract and simultaneously selling short the stock index, the investor can profit from the price discrepancy. This is known as cash-and-carry arbitrage, where the investor goes long in the cheaper asset (futures contract) and short in the more expensive asset (stock index) to capture the price difference.

75. Answer: D) All of the above. The price of a call option on a stock is influenced by multiple factors. The stock's volatility, or the degree of price fluctuation, affects the option's value. Higher volatility generally leads to higher option prices. Additionally, the stock's dividend yield plays a role. If the stock pays dividends, the option's price may be adjusted downward to account for the expected dividend payments. Lastly, the risk-free interest rate impacts the option price. Higher interest rates tend to increase the option's value. Therefore, all of the factors mentioned in the options—volatility, dividend yield, and risk-free interest rate—affect the price of a call option on a stock.

76. Answer: B) When there is a negative correlation between futures prices and interest rates. When futures prices and interest rates exhibit a negative correlation, the pricing of forwards and futures will diverge. Specifically, the negative correlation makes forwards more attractive than futures when considering the long position.

77. Answer: A) The company will make a net payment. When the fixed rate is higher than the expected floating rate, the company will make a net payment in an interest rate swap.

This is because the company is obligated to pay the fixed rate, which exceeds the expected floating rate it receives.

78. Answer: B) Intrinsic value: $10, Time value: $0. The intrinsic value of a call option is the difference between the stock price and the strike price when the stock price is above the strike price. In this case, the intrinsic value is $60 - $50 = $10. The time value is the difference between the premium and the intrinsic value. Here, the time value is $3 - $10 = -$7. However, the time value cannot be negative, so it is considered to be zero.

79. Answer: C). Buy a put option and sell the underlying asset. To replicate the payoff of a call option using put options and other securities, an investor needs to create a position that mimics the upside potential of the call option. According to put-call parity, the relationship between call and put options is given by the formula:
Call Option = Put Option + Underlying Asset - Present Value of Exercise Price
By rearranging the formula, we can replicate the call option payoff by buying a put option and selling the underlying asset.
Option C, "Buy a put option and sell the underlying asset," achieves this replication strategy. By buying a put option, the investor gains the right to sell the underlying asset at a predetermined price (the exercise price). By selling the underlying asset, the investor benefits from a decline in the asset's price, which offsets the potential loss from the put option.

80. Answer: A) $14.29
Using the one-period binomial model:
S_up = $50 * (1 + 0.6) = $50 * 1.6 = $80
S_down = $50 * (1 - 0.6) = $50 * 0.4 = $20
Next, calculate the expected value of the call option:
Call Value = [p * Max(0, S_up - X)] + [(1 - p) * Max(0, S_down - X)] / (1 + r)
Call Value = [0.6 * Max(0, $80 - $55)] + [0.4 * Max(0, $20 - $55)] / (1 + 0.05)
Call Value = [0.6 * Max(0, $25)] + [0.4 * Max(0, -$35)] / 1.05

Call Value = [0.6 * $25] + [0.4 * $0] / 1.05
Call Value = $15 + $0 / 1.05
Call Value = $15 / 1.05
Call Value = $14.29

81. Answer: B) Real estate. Real estate investments are typically characterized by a fixed term, illiquidity, and a focus on capital preservation. They involve investing in properties such as residential, commercial, or industrial buildings.

82. Answer: A) Management fees and carried interest. Private equity investments commonly use a compensation structure that includes management fees and carried interest. Management fees are charged by the private equity firm for managing the investment, while carried interest represents the share of profits that the firm receives upon successful realization of the investment.

83. Answer: B) $22,000
Management fee = 2% * $500,000 = $10,000
Profit = 12% * $500,000 = $60,000
Performance fee = 20% * $60,000 = $12,000
Total fees paid = Management fee + Performance fee = $10,000 + $12,000 = $22,000

84. Answer: C) Hedge funds. A lock-up period refers to a predetermined period during which investors are restricted from redeeming or selling their investment in a fund. Hedge funds commonly impose lock-up periods to align the interests of investors with the fund manager and prevent excessive withdrawals during short-term market fluctuations.

85. Answer: C) $1,488,320
Total investment value = Initial capital commitment * (1 + Return)^Holding period
Total investment value = $1,000,000 * (1 + 20%)^5
Total investment value = $1,000,000 * 1.20^5
Total investment value = $1,000,000 * 1.48832
Total investment value ≈ $1,488,320

86. Answer: D) Active involvement in portfolio companies. Private equity investments involve acquiring equity ownership in privately-held companies. One of the key characteristics of private equity is the active involvement of the investors or private equity firms in the management and

strategic decisions of the portfolio companies. This active engagement aims to enhance the value of the invested companies and maximize returns.
87. Answer: C) Market risk. Infrastructure investments, such as toll roads, airports, and utilities, are often characterized by stable cash flows and long-term contracts. Unlike traditional asset classes, infrastructure investments are less exposed to market risk because they are based on long-term agreements or regulated pricing structures. However, infrastructure investments still face risks such as regulatory risk, construction risk, and managerial risk.
88. Answer: D. Real estate. Real estate is an asset class that has the potential to provide inflation hedging benefits. As property values and rental income tend to increase with inflation, real estate investments can act as a hedge against inflation. Additionally, real estate investments often generate stable cash flows through rental income, making them attractive for income-focused investors.
89. Answer: D) Use of macroeconomic analysis and trends. Hedge funds employing a global macro strategy focus on macroeconomic analysis and trends to make investment decisions. These funds take positions based on anticipated macroeconomic events, such as changes in interest rates, exchange rates, or global economic trends. They aim to generate returns by correctly predicting and taking advantage of large-scale economic shifts. High portfolio turnover, focus on short-term trading, and bottom-up stock picking are more commonly associated with other hedge fund strategies, such as equity-focused or event-driven strategies.
90. Answer: A) Private equity. Private equity investments are typically characterized by longer lock-up periods and limited liquidity. Private equity funds invest in privately held companies and often have a long-term investment horizon. Investors in private equity funds commit their capital for a specific period, known as the lock-up period, during which they cannot easily redeem or sell their investment. This illiquidity is due to the nature of private equity investments, which involve direct ownership in private companies that are not publicly traded.

Printed in Great Britain
by Amazon